Love, Love, Love

COWLEY PUBLICATIONS is a ministry of the brothers of the
Society of Saint John the Evangelist, a monastic order in the
Episcopal Church. Our mission is to provide books and resources
for those seeking spiritual and theological formation. COWLEY
PUBLICATIONS is committed to de   new generation
of writers and teachers who will en
pray in new ways about spiritual
future.

Love, Love, Love

AND OTHER ESSAYS

Light Reflections on Love, Life, and Death

Charles Taliaferro

Cowley Publications
CAMBRIDGE, MASSACHUSETTS

Published in the United States of America by Cowley Publications, a division of the Society of Saint John the Evangelist. No portion of this book may be reproduced, stored in or introduced into a retrieval system, or transmitted, in any form or by any means—including photocopying—without the prior written permission of Cowley Publications, except in the case of brief quotations embedded in critical articles and reviews.

Library of Congress Cataloging-in-Publication Data:

Taliaferro, Charles.
    Love, love, love and other essays : light reflections on love, life, and death / Charles Taliaferro.
        p.   cm.
    Includes bibliographical references.
    ISBN-10: 1-56101-242-4   ISBN-13: 978-1-56101-242-8 (pbk. : alk. paper)
    1. Love.   I. Title.
    BD436.T255 2006
    177'.7—dc22   2005033487

Cover design: Gary Ragaglia
Cover art: Jil Evans, *Tiepolo's Cloud #24* (detail), (34" × 28", oil, 2001).
Collection of Lois Conner.
Text design: Wendy Holdman

This book was printed in the United States of America on acid-free paper.

Cowley Publications
4 Brattle Street
Cambridge, Massachusetts 02138
800-225-1534 • www.cowley.org

"Space is the Whom our loves are needed by,
Time is our choice of How to love and Why."

W. H. Auden (1907–1973)
For the Time Being—
"A Christmas Oratorio"

"The World was all before them, where to choose
Their place of rest, and Providence their guide:
They hand in hand with wandering steps and slow,
Through Eden took thir solitarie way."

John Milton (1608–1674)
Paradise Lost, Book XII, 646–649

"Let us love, dear love,
Lyke as we ought
Love is the Lesson
That the Lord us taught."

Edmund Spenser (1552–1599)
Easter Sonnett

Table of Contents

Acknowledgments

———

I THANK JIL EVANS FOR HER SUPPORT AND HER COMMENTS on earlier drafts of these essays. I am also deeply grateful to Paula Schanilec, Sarah Lauer, Kira Obolensky, Marc Nieson, Katie Solomonson, Carol Strait, David Onan, Glenn Gordon, Beckie Judge, Randy Jennings, Trish McElroy, Phil Docken, Dan Sinykin, Kristen Rau, Thomas Carson, Paul Reasoner, Anthony Rudd, Jason Zencka and Jennifer Cross. I am also very grateful for Kelly Robbins's editorial advice and assistance. My gratitude is no mere courteous nod of the head, but an immense appreciation of the support, wit, and insights of these dear friends.

Past readers whose support has been very important include Jeanette Zwart, Gary Wicks, Diana Postlethwaite, David Booth, Gordon Marino, Robert Entenmann, Pat Quade, Ed Langerak, George Holt, Bonnie Sherman, Cleo Granneman, Richard Kyle.

The first essay, "A Professor's Tale," is dedicated to David Oppegaard, as well as to Leanne and Michael, Susan and Charles with thanks to Thomas Carson. "Going Up? The Lighter Side of Christian Mysticism" is for Rick Taylor ("Great Mind") and Michel LeGall. The last three essays are written in love and gratitude for my father. "Shipwrecks and Immortality" is dedicated to my colleague William Narum, and "Hello Tiepelo" is for Dore Ashton and in loving memory of Matti Megged. "A Modest Defense of Magic" was inspired by the Polichs of Dover Street and the essay on Russia is for Eleonore and Monica Stump. "A Student's Tale" is dedicated to Sarah Lauer, and "Dr. Visitor" is for Susan Killoran. I am deeply indebted to Michael Wilt and to Father Curtis Almquist, SSJE, for this opportunity to write *Love, Love, Love And Other Essays* for Cowley Publications. "The Virtues of the Cloister" is a tribute to SSJE spirituality. I am also very grateful to the Harvard Divinity School student and Cowley Publications associate Scott Neely for his expert advice, good humor, and work on this manuscript. These essays were finally revised, and three of them composed, at Harris Manchester College, Oxford University. I am grateful to Reverend Dr. Ralph Waller and the fellows of the college for their gracious hospitality.

Many of the essays appear here for the first time, though, as noted in the introduction that follows, many of them were also first written in particular settings (e.g., immediately following the death of a senator) and have been circulated in different forums. "It's Waterloo, Baby!" appears in *Understanding Dying, Death, and Bereavement,* for example. And "Jury Duty with James Bond" was published in a journal (*The Challenger*) for judges, clerks, probation officers, and lawyers. I wrote the Bond essay after serving on a jury and sent it to Judge Andrew W. Danielson, who presided at the trial in the Fourth Judicial District Court in the State of Minnesota. In correspondence he wrote, "Humor is in somewhat short supply when it comes to courtroom matters. It is not necessarily in short supply when attorneys and Judges get together to discuss various matters but usually what goes on in the courtroom is somewhat more restrained. I personally think that there is a place in the courtroom for humor also as long as the serious nature of the proceedings is retained." Indeed. I agree with Judge Danielson and thank him and all others who have encouraged these light essays on serious proceedings that range from coping with a shipwreck to apologizing for forging a letter.

Charles Taliaferro
St. Olaf College
Northfield, Minnesota

An Introduction

THERE IS A SPLENDID PHRASE TO DESCRIBE A WORK OF ART that is created in particular circumstances: such work is made *in situ.* In a sense, these essays were each written *in situ,* occasioned by specific events that are odd or embarrassing, like sleepwalking nearly naked late at night in a major metropolitan hotel, or tragic, like the death of a parent. And some were occasioned by ordinary yet troubling events, like serving on a jury. But they were also written in an effort to touch on wide themes, such as the pathetic futility of vanity, the awakening of faith, and the surprising consolation and joy found in friendship. The overall goal of this collection is the exploration of different aspects of love.

These forty-three essays are sorted into three groups. The first set of essays introduces a variety of themes about friendship and compassion (among other things). Some of these essays involve the concept of divine love that was wonderfully described by the late medieval French mystic, Hugh of St. Victor:

> That love is unique but not private, alone but not
> isolated, shared but not divided, both communal and
> individual, a singular love of all and a total love of each,
> not decreased by sharing nor diminished by use; not
> aging in time, ever old, ever new; desirable to anticipate,

sweet to experience, eternal in its fruits, full of delight, restoring and satisfying, never growing tiresome.

While the first set of essays takes its cue from personal events, the second is more oriented to public, political, and cultural matters. I hope these essays further Hugh of St. Victor's portrait of divine love in political, literary, and cultural terms. The final three essays focus on a subject that is personal, but not unique or isolated: the illness and death of a parent.

A few words are in order about the essay format itself. I fell in love with short works of what is now called "creative nonfiction" in my early twenties when I was in graduate school working on a sprawling dissertation. Dr. Samuel Johnson's famous comment on a classic poem ("none wished it longer") could without any doubt apply to my dissertation, and I found myself seeking refuge in literature that was quite the opposite: I wanted work that I wished was longer. I relished short essays that are suggestive, tantalizing, and economic. I developed some sympathy with G. K. Chesterton's judgment: "It may, perhaps be wondered whether one could possibly say a worse thing of anybody than that he had said 'the last word' on a subject. A man who says the last word on a subject ought to be killed. He is a murderer; he has slain a topic. The best kind of critic draws attention not to the finality of a thing, but to its infinity. Instead of closing a question, he opens a hundred."

While I have enjoyed many essayists over many years, especially W. H. Auden, T. S. Eliot, Dorothy Sayers, C. S. Lewis, and George Orwell, my all-time favorite remains G. K. Chesterton (1874–1936). With Chesterton, something as commonplace as watching a tree swaying in the wind at night or chasing after his hat in a railway station could be the start of a meditation on the meaning of adventures or the Trinity. He convinced me that almost any event in life can be a poignant occasion for serious thought and action. For example: "I have never understood," he wrote, "what people mean by domesticity being tame; it seems to me one of the wildest adventures. But if you wish to see how high and harsh and fantastic an adventure it is, consider only the actual structure of a house itself. A man may march up in a rather bored way to bed, but at least he is mounting to a height from which he could kill himself."

When I completed graduate training and came to St. Olaf College in Minnesota as a professor of philosophy, I began writing up experiences and reflections *in situ* for friends and my community at large. *Love, Love, Love And Other Essays* was written between 2000 and 2005. The work is, in part, inspired by Chesterton's philosophy and style and so one of the essays, "A Very Large, Magical Victorian," is a tribute to Chesterton's work.

I prize exchange. While I do sometimes offer lectures in my role as a college professor, my preferred context is always the spontaneity of conversation. Should any of these essays occasion the desire to begin an exchange, I would welcome the opportunity to correspond.

PART ONE

Divine Love in Ordinary Time

A Professor's Tale

I GREW UP ON STORIES OF HIGH ADVENTURE AROUND A kitchen table where my dad and my brothers talked of mountain climbing, stunt flying, crossing the Atlantic in a 30-foot sailboat with an airline pilot, Word War II and Vietnam, and daredevil finances. As a college professor I, too, have adventures but, from the outside, they sometimes seem more like what my bothers would call *inconveniences*. Last month I received an email: "Steve [the editor] is upset! The deadline has passed and the footnotes are a catastrophe!" I jumped in the car, turned on some heroic, do-or-die music, pushed the speed limit and went to the library. I ran through the stacks, checking journals, and phoned two colleagues and a student worker. The frenzy ended with a call to Fed Ex, and the revised manuscript was on its way to England—rush charges applied. Sweating, exhausted, and relieved, I was also keenly aware that the events of the day did not compete with Dad's near-death experience at over 14,000 feet on the Matterhorn in the Swiss Alps.

You may not need an oxygen mask to undertake conventional college teaching but, if you don't mind a mixture of metaphors, it does have its share of mountains, oceans, warfare, and peace. There are the extraordinary times when a student is in profound trouble, but there are also more subtle, quiet cases when life-changing decisions are made. And most, if not all, of us care passionately about this. Last week a colleague thought his class was a complete disaster. Rather than attribute this to seniors contemplating spring break, he went to the office, locked the door, turned off the lights, wrapped himself in his academic gown, and prayed that God would take his life. He had to admit later that this was "melodramatic," but (for better or worse) this sort of thing happens with some regularity and, on the flip side, a successful class can send one joyfully to the moon. However, for all the agony and ecstasy, stories of college classroom adventures are admittedly no match for tales of wing walking on a biplane in the Grand Canyon.

In class I once accidentally cut my hand. Without realizing that this had opened a prior wound causing extensive bleeding, I proceeded to wipe my forehead and stroke my chin, smearing blood all over my face in front of about thirty students in an ethics class. The combination of horror and humor may have boosted enrollment for the next term but, at the end of the day, the whole event felt like an appalling, amateur re-enactment of the closing scenes of *Apocalypse Now*. An even worse case of an "adventure": For the first meeting of a course on the philosophy of human nature, I thought it would be exciting to discuss human anatomy using a visual aid. Just before class, a colleague from the psychology department sent me a plastic tub with three human brains floating in formaldehyde. Class got off to an excellent start, but soon my "expertise" on brain anatomy was exhausted, and I became utterly disoriented when an enthusiastic non-pre-med student suggested it would be "illuminating" to carry out an informal, "creative" dissection. Another student proposed that we should requisition to get a whole cadaver to work on throughout the term. Soon the entire class plunged into a state of sadness ("Where did these brains come from?") and nausea (due to the fumes).

These morbid fiascos do not even match a more action-packed calamity involving a colleague who used to smoke in class back in the day. He once flipped a lit cigarette into a wastebasket full of paper, which started smoldering a few minutes later. He then put his foot into the large metal basket in an attempt to extinguish what was slowly becoming a small fire. Unfortunately, his foot got stuck. He created a racket banging the wastebasket up and down on the tile floor trying to extract his foot from the flames. Thankfully, these types of events are at the margins of college life.

A very different story with a very different point of view from just outside the classroom: David, a student, came into my office one day. His mother had died the term before. He had to fill out a form. "Mind if I do this here?" Be my guest. He came to a question about his mother. "You know, this is the first time I have had to write the word *deceased*." Silence. "Does the pain ever stop?" he asked. I will not tell you what I said, partly because it was completely clumsy and certainly less than brilliant. But being there then was worth sailing the ocean.

Jury Duty with James Bond

———•———

WHEN I RECEIVED A NOTICE FOR JURY DUTY IN HENNEPIN County in Minneapolis, I also received lots of advice from friends on how to avoid serving. I was tempted to look for an escape route after studying *A Handbook for Trial Jurors.* Under the heading "Benefits of Jury Service," I read: "You may have had an opportunity to play a leading role in a real life drama." Life has often seemed to me to be a little *too* dramatic. The handbook also noted, "When you are chosen as a juror, for a short time you are a part of the government machinery of this state." I have never desired to be part of a machine! (I would have responded more positively to a metaphor involving gardens or plants.) Still, after arriving for jury duty on an icy January morning and listening to a speech on Justice and the Constitution, I was ready for ten days of service.

After one day of simply waiting to be called, I was part of a wave of twenty-four people sent up to the nineteenth floor of the Hennepin County District Court. I was placed under oath to tell the truth (so help me God) and was questioned by a judge and two attorneys to determine whether I should be selected as one of twelve jurors. "Occupation?" College professor. "Subject?" Philosophy. "What is your educational background?" I have a B.A., three masters degrees, and a Ph.D. "Do students find your credentials intimidating?" No. They usually assume they know more than me. "Are you a problem-solver?" I don't mean to be difficult, but I am not sure what you mean. "Do you like to do jigsaw puzzles?" I suppose so, though I'm not very good. I tend to find individual pieces very interesting and have a difficult time putting them together. "Are you a leader or a follower?" To be honest, I don't think of myself as either. "Do you have any favorite films or television shows about law?" Yes. *The Verdict* and *Law and Order.* "You realize that *Law and Order* moves at a fast pace and gives the impression that trials are over quickly." I understand. "Do you ever read mysteries?" Yes. "Do you ever skip ahead to see who did 'it'?" Oh dear. . . . At this point, I put my head in my hands and confessed: Yes. I do. Many of my fellow prospective jurors either laughed or looked at me with a mock-scolding expression. Evidently I was not thereby disqualified, for I was selected to serve on the jury.

I love mysteries, especially espionage stories, but I don't read them for suspense. I read the least suspenseful espionage stories available. At the time of the trial I was reading a glossy blue book with the bright title *James Bond in Win, Lose or Die* by John Gardner. From the first page you know that the hero will prevail. I was embarrassed to have a Bond novel with me, so I tried to disguise it by placing it inside a dull-looking textbook. Ian Fleming invented the character of Bond, and, after Fleming's death in 1964, Gardner (as well as a few other writers) continued to write up adventures for Bond. In Gardner's novels Bond is still the most successful anti-terrorist spy since the Second World War, but he is less sexist. He even has a tendency to committed relationships and citing Churchill; there is no sadism, but instead some sentimentality and the occasional prayer. Two examples: "'James? . . . Love me?' He held her. 'I love you very much,' and he realized he meant it." Or even: "'We have a hymn,' Bond unexpectedly heard himself say, 'It is a prayer. *Oh hear us when we cry to Thee, for those in peril on the sea.*'" At the time I found such Bond books the ideal escape literature, and I found J. R. R. Tolkien's defense of escape literature authoritative (those who oppose escape literature are probably jailers). But for all that, I turned red when a juror discovered me reading the book. She announced the title to three other jurors and then said, "He's just like us!"

Our jury was charged with judging a case involving a relationship gone bad. "Isaac" and "Becky" quarreled. Allegedly, Isaac threatened Becky, menaced others at a bar, and then used his motorcycle in an unsuccessful effort to run over two people in a parking lot. So the charges were *Assault* and *Making Terrorist Threats*. The trial included a massive amount of testimony, diagrams, and objections. The lengthy, repetitive questioning would have tried the patience of Job. I had to force myself to concentrate on the details, as I felt a growing mix of sadness and wistful fantasy: Why didn't you two get along? You both seem intelligent, healthy, clear, and concerned with telling the truth (now, anyway). Well? I must have looked disheartened because a juror nudged me and asked, "And how is Mr. Bond today?"

The trial lasted five days, including six hours of jury deliberation. Much of the event felt completely unscripted; you are thrown together with eleven people you have never met before and, chances are, will not see again. There was serious disagreement, hurt feelings, and misunderstanding. There was also a good sense of humor, collaboration, and careful reflection. During our deliberations we were required to eat together. There were some cigarette breaks, but these were not solitary affairs. All twelve of us, along with two deputies, had to accompany the smokers when they lit up. One juror told another he respected her even though they disagreed. She replied that the respect was mutual.

On the fifth day we filed into the courtroom with our verdict. Guilty. Isaac put his head in his hands. I felt sick to my stomach. We were polled. "Is this your verdict?" Answer: Yes. I was only half prepared for the solidity of our decision. The conviction felt heavy and painful. There was no pleasure in it.

Since the trial I have been reading less about agent 007. Instead, I have been reading Charles Dickens. I think this is because Dickens developed all the characters of his novels, even the villains, on an ocean of sympathy. Rakes and ne'er-do-wells are sketched with moral insight and good-natured irony. Dickens saw beauty and humor where we might see only banality and ugliness. Underneath his narratives, there is a contagious love of people and an earnest desire for the redemption of everyone, not just "the elect." I believe he would have loved Isaac and Becky.

Apart from switching authors, the other thing that has changed in my life since the trial involves prayer. I now pray for the eleven other jurors, the judge, the witnesses, the attorneys, Isaac, Becky, and those in peril in Hennepin County District Court.

Shipwrecks and Immortality

THERE IS A SAYING THAT ALL PHILOSOPHERS ARE SAD (*omnes philosophi tristes*). I am not convinced of that, but I am convinced that some laughing philosophers are a bit chilling. Democritus (460–370 BCE) was known as the "laughing philosopher" because, in part, he laughed at death. But I am not sure why death should be so funny or liberating considering that, if Democritus is right, death involves complete and utter annihilation. I certainly hope Democritus was not like a scary, old philosopher I once knew in Iowa who said he took great pleasure in watching the best minds of his generation pass into oblivion. In any event, whatever success I have had in beating back cosmic despair came about in a way that is quite different from Democritus and the scary professor from Iowa. One of the most recent moments of relief came after a terrible shipwreck.

In November 1997 my first book published by Blackwell (*Contemporary Philosophy of Religion*) was placed on board the *MSC Carla* in LeHavre, France. The three thousand copies of my book were among a total of roughly half a million books and thousands of cases of vintage wine. The voyage, which was to be nonstop from LeHavre to Boston, was doomed. On November 25, the crew of thirty-four encountered violent storms off the mid-Atlantic Portuguese Azores Islands with waves up to ten meters high and gale-force winds. The vessel was torn in two 110 miles north of São Miguel Island, requiring a rescue operation by the Portuguese Air Force. Responding to an emergency SOS radio signal, a helicopter was dispatched and rescued twenty-one of the crewmen, while those remaining stayed in the stern of the vessel, attempting to save its cargo. The weather deteriorated rapidly. Several containers were jettisoned in an effort to stay afloat. A Liberian-registered vessel arrived in the area to assist. At the end of the day, the rest of the boat sank, its cargo lost (including some nuclear material in three cesium capsules inside medical equipment) and the remaining crew taken by helicopter to the Portuguese Air Base 4 at Lajes. No lives were lost. Thank God! But somewhere on the ocean floor of the North Atlantic you will find 500,000 books and some fine wine.

The news of the shipwreck was not widespread. I gathered the above details from shipping and insurance companies. The longest formal published article on the catastrophe was in *The Wine Spectator*.

Colleagues on my campus responded with various explanations (e.g., God did not like your book). But the best reply came in an Under the Sea Party put on by two colleagues, Tony and Beckie. They digitally copied and reduced the book jacket and made dozens of tiny replicas of *Contemporary Philosophy of Religion* which they placed in a huge aquarium filled with little fish and a plastic scuba diver. They also excerpted blurbs from the back cover of the book like "Taliaferro covers both front burner and back burner issues," which they then framed next to reproductions of characters such as the lobster from the Walt Disney movie *The Little Mermaid*. They served a great deal of wonderful Portuguese port, which we enjoyed while listening to Handel's "Water Works."

One other story of challenging despair: My colleague Bill is dying. He was declared "terminal" six months ago (cancer) but as I write this he is still with us. I have always thought of him as our C. S. Lewis, the Oxford and then Cambridge don, scholar, author of children's books, man of faith and philosophy. Bill has always given my colleagues and me the sense that this world is a "shadowland," and that on the other side there is no oblivion, but something more akin to the merriment of friendship. Some of us have been taking turns visiting Bill and driving him to one of his favorite destinations: Dairy Queen. When I took Bill out for his ice cream last month I wore my formal academic robe. It is not every day that you get to take a C. S. Lewis out for a "blizzard" at Dairy Queen.

When I last paid Bill a visit I thought again about the *MSC Carla,* in part because I felt that I was watching another vessel in trouble. Though still awake and lucid, Bill was no longer able to read, the ice cream outings had to be canceled, and his library was being broken up. It almost seemed as though books were being thrown overboard to lighten the load. No helicopter was coming to save him. Still, there was something else very much like a rescue going on in the room, something that made me think about "the other side."

Bill was not alone. A former student, maybe 50 years old, balding but still youthful-looking, was beside him. Bill and his wife had befriended him during his first year in college, inviting him and other students to their home for conversation, both philosophical and personal, and some meals. "You were a *great* teacher," the student said, clearly and deliberately. Bill's eyes brightened. If I were on my deathbed I would probably have said, "Thank you," or, worse, "Please, tell me more!" Instead, Bill said, "We did have fun, didn't we?"

Not all philosophers are sad. I don't think Democritus' laugh could possibly have been as full and deep as Bill's. Being able to glimpse some of Bill's faith and hope feels like finding a gift. It's as though I am deep underwater scuba diving, admiring lobsters crawling on the ocean floor when suddenly, without warning, I come across some vintage wine.

Dr. Visitor

THE SHOUTING WAS AMAZING. ALMOST FROM THE START, the three-day conference in Philadelphia was pandemonium in the traditional sense of the word (in *Paradise Lost* Milton's name for the abode of the demons is "pandemonium"). The gathering included several neuroscientists, a handful of philosophers, and a psychoanalyst who was convinced that two other attendees had no integrity. In the course of telling one of the neurologists that he was a liar, the analyst bit off the prongs of his plastic fork, then continued to shout violently as he gestured with the mangled utensil. I tried to intervene by noting that we were all *visitors*. I was relying on what I thought was an ongoing as well as ancient practice (going back at least to Homer) in which there is a strict canon of respect governing the guest-host relationship. I even attempted to capture the spirit of hospitality by presenting our hosts with a flowery plant. The offering was accepted, but despite the fact that it became known as "the benevolent plant," there was no sign of *any* benevolence among the warring parties. As the leader of the conference told me on the second day of meetings, "We now have good empirical data that the presence of flowers does not lessen hostility." I can only imagine what it was like for the analyst and the "lying" neuroscientist to share a cab to the airport when the conference came to a merciful end.

There are certainly advantages to being a visitor. For example, during a stay at Oxford University, it usually becomes clear that guests enjoy a kind of non-combatant status. We visitors are generally not considered competitors for the rare academic appointment or prestigious chairs. We also get invited to some nice meals even though they are occasionally accompanied by a small side of embarrassment: A professor invited me out to dinner. When I offered to pick up the bill, I was told, "Oh, no. It's my treat because you don't belong here." I mumbled something about *trying* to belong at Oxford, but was interrupted by the clanging of the cash register.

Eventually, I acquired an appropriate nickname. A parcel was sent to me at Oxford addressed: "For Dr. Charles Taliaferro Visitor." The bursar posted a general notice: "A package has arrived for Dr. Visitor." Sheepishly, I retrieved the parcel and was (temporarily) stuck with the "affectionate" nickname.

At my home institution (St. Olaf College) back in the States, I sometimes seek to retain the sensibility of a visitor. In my experience, the professors who have the most trouble retiring are those who act as though they own their office, classes, students, and even some part of the institution itself. It becomes very difficult for them to let go, and their outlook can be especially dark when they believe they have an irrevocable, imperial right to appoint their successor. If I am alive long enough to retire, I shall probably make a complete mess of things. I hope, however, that by acting like a visitor now, I can reduce the feeling that retirement involves a baffling disenfranchisement and the preposterous, unjust occupation of one's current office by an unwelcome young stranger.

Hosting visitors has obvious liabilities. There is a biblical injunction to entertain strangers on the grounds that some of them may be angels ("Be not forgetful to entertain strangers: for thereby some have entertained angels unawares." Hebrews 13:2, KJV). Of course the opposite is also true, and you may inadvertently wind up entertaining demons. For this reason I think there is a special pleasure and fitting sense of respect and gratitude when someone takes the risk of welcoming you into their library, institution, or home. You may seem, and actually turn out to be, civil and kind, but any host who truly welcomes you is taking a risk that you may completely break down and, in between curses, start disfiguring the eating utensils.

The librarian at Oxford who greeted my wife, Jil Evans, and me was the exact opposite of the Philadelphia demons. Susan knew how an institution like Oxford could have its inside and outside. We were interested in eighteenth-century art. "If you came here with that interest twenty years ago," said Susan, "I would have said, 'Not here, darlings.'" As it turns out, we were now in the right place, for Susan showed us how to access an enviable stash of books and prints. Straight away I got the distinct feeling that we were considered angels (until further notice). As a good host, she also seemed to know how to take care of demons and witches. Perhaps as a warning, she told us—with a wink and a smile—that the natural history museum down the street had an exhibit that included a witch who had been captured in a bottle. I wondered whether this observation was code for "make sure you don't have overdue books." In any event, her warm welcome—so much more effective than the benevolent plant in Philadelphia—made us feel that we belonged, not despite the fact that we were visitors, but because we were visitors.

Do Not Hug a Tree on a Job Interview Unless There Is a Very Good Reason for Doing So

EARLY IN THE MORNING, I SOMETIMES WALK OUR DOG with a neighbor who, from time to time, hugs a tree. For some reason, we both find this funny. I have often thought it comical due to its sheer unmotivated absurdity. The right time and place for such behavior, however, is important.

One summer I was flown out to Princeton Theological Seminary to be interviewed for a chair of philosophy. At dawn on a Saturday morning, I was strolling across campus on my way to the place where, in another hour, I would meet Professor J. Wentzel van Huyssteen, a prominent philosopher and theologian who has contributed first-rate work on the relationship of science and religion. I was nervous. There, in front of me, was a lovely huge tree. I saw no one. Convinced I was completely unobserved, I approached the tree and gave it a big hug.

When the professor met me later his line of inquiry worried me. "Ah, Charles, my wife and I saw you enjoying a walk on campus." Silence. "We have a very nice campus, don't you think?" Yes, I replied. "And Princeton has some very nice trees." I changed the subject, and the conversation continued amicably. To this day, I do not know whether the professor (or anyone else) saw what I did. If he did see me hug the tree, it evidently did not secure me the job. Some months later (the following spring, with the trees just starting to come into fresh growth) I was told the search for a new chair was suspended due to funding problems.

I have had a long time to ponder why I hugged that tree. The best I have come up with is as follows: "Yes, professor, I did hug that tree. But of course that was because I was meditating on the biblical text, Proverbs 3:18." This "justification" is still a bit of a stretch. The verse reads, "[Wisdom] is a tree of life to those who lay hold of her; / those who hold her fast are called happy." But while this text speaks directly in favor of holding wisdom like a tree, it is another matter to recommend holding a tree like wisdom.

Whether the tree-hugging episode cost me a job or not, it did help pave the way to an experience I do not (yet) regret. Several years ago, I was in a museum in Russia where I saw an icon of the Trinity. It was behind glass. I believe it was either the original or a copy of Andrei Rublev's fifteenth-century masterpiece *Trinity*. A museum worker came up to it, knelt, and kissed the glass casing. She observed a minute of silence and then moved on. I wanted to join her, but I was too embarrassed. After the encounter with that tree at Princeton, however, I have been a little bolder.

At the British Museum in London, there is a reliquary of Thomas à Becket, the Archbishop of Canterbury who was martyred in 1170. He heroically held his ground by retaining the integrity of the Church against the manipulative control of his former friend King Henry II, who was complicit in St. Thomas's assassination. The relics of this saint were highly prized in the medieval period, and they were the key reason for pilgrims to travel to Canterbury—as recounted in Chaucer's *Canterbury Tales*. Chaucer's tales are, I think, a splendid mix of the sacred and the profane, a celebration of God and the flesh.

As C. S. Lewis once pointed out, "It is a lesson worth learning, how Chaucer can so triumphantly celebrate the flesh without becoming either delirious or pornographic." Lewis describes Chaucer's prose as being deeply rooted in the earth, like a colossal tree with branches that reach up to heaven. At 3:00 in the afternoon in the museum, I wondered whether I might venerate Becket in the tradition of Chaucer and the Russian museum worker.

Although emboldened by the affair with the tree, I was not going to attempt hugging the reliquary or go for a full prostration on the floor. Kissing the glass case was not going to be an option. Kissing an icon is an established custom in the Russian Orthodox Church, whereas there is nothing remotely similar governing the behavior of American tourists approaching medieval objects in the museums of London. While I still recommend not hugging a tree before, during, or after a job interview, the fiasco did help relax the cultural mandate of remaining completely aloof and detached in the presence of St. Thomas's remains. I was carrying a bag, which I then placed on the floor. To anyone looking on, I was a weary traveler taking a break, kneeling on the floor for about a minute in order to sort through my backpack.

Drugs, a Bear, and an Owl: A Testimony

DURING A PRESENTATION IN CLASS THIS WEEK, A STU-dent mentioned in passing that the founder of psychoanalysis, Sigmund Freud, took an "inordinate" amount of cocaine. This suggested to me that the student thought that cocaine might be used in a fashion that was balanced, healthy, and altogether ordinary.

For me and a handful of friends in our first year of college in Vermont, using drugs (principally psychoactive substances like LSD-25, mescaline, psilocybin, cannabis sativa, stropharia cubensis, and dimethyltryptamine rather than cocaine) was often inordinate. And while the results were sometimes amusing in an eerie way (I occasionally hallucinated little people baking cookies or playing tennis), things inevitably ended (for us) very, very badly. My girlfriend at the time became addicted to heroin; a close friend was killed in one of those "suspicious" car accidents (was it an accident or a suicide?). Recovery for me began with two months in a Christian community in the county of Hampshire in south central England. In retrospect, I am still amazed that I came out on the other side feeling younger, not older. It was as though I was younger at 20 than I was at 17 or 18. I suspect part of this involved not just a shift in goals and intention, but even a shift when it came to humor.

G. K. Chesterton proposed that humor, at its best, requires some stable, sane background. *Alice in Wonderland* is only funny when you assume that rabbits don't rush around with clocks, talking and so on. But lose that, as I did on mescaline while looking at Lewis Carroll's lovely book on a library floor during my freshman year, and the humor is gone. Looking back, I think that my friends and I probably had less sense of humor than the glum character Gollum in *The Lord of the Rings.* For example: Along with two friends, I would pretend that the people I spoke with were gradually but increasingly being covered in snow. When they were completely covered with (imaginary) snow we moved on. Another case: I once thought it was terribly funny to dress in a black cape and hat, eating strawberries for a whole day in front of the local library. This probably just scared children (and would have delighted Gollum). A final example: Years later, I listened to a tape of an LSD trip I took when I was 18. At the very heart of "the trip" my friend and I came to the conclusion that "things take up space." Today, I still find space, as a topic, fascinating, but I now pursue it through philosophy and science rather than with a variety of psychotropic drugs.

I believe that my initial attraction to hallucinogens bordered on the religious. As a teenager, I was convinced by Aldous Huxley's stunning accounts of the uses of mescaline in his classic *The Doors of Perception:*

> I was seeing what Adam had seen on the morning of
> creation—the miracle, moment by moment, of naked
> existence . . . flowers shining with their own inner light
> and all but quivering under the pressure of the signifi-
> cance with which they were charged. . . . Words like
> 'grace' and 'transfiguration' came to mind. . . .

What could possibly go wrong? At least two things for me. First, I found it hard to come up with healthy, balanced, ordinate dosages. Second, in the end, the use of psychedelics made me more focused on the doors of perception than on what was out there, independent of myself, to perceive. There is a great line from the Beatles' *Sergeant Pepper* album: "What do you see when you turn out the lights? I cannot tell you, but I know it's mine." With or without the lights, I was seeing projections of my own visual library (and unless you adore watching tennis-playing pastry chefs, the imagery was not spectacular). In short, rather than being like Adam seeing creation afresh, I was seeing creation like Eve in John Milton's *Paradise Lost*. She became more interested in seeing her own reflection (Book IV), and her self-preoccupation paved the way for the Fall (Book IX).

Recovery for me involved a kind of falling in love with the world outside me. One counselor put the point in a corny phrase: *Better to have love-induced rather than drug-induced experiences.*

In the Christian English community where I stayed, I am sure there were serious doubts about my progress. For some reason, I developed a temporary love for knitting; I liked the rhythm and skill involved. I also had a specific project. Before leaving for England, a friend from school had given me a teddy bear (this was partly inspired by *Brideshead Revisited;* the main character, Sebastian, goes to college with a teddy bear named Aloysius, the patron saint of Catholic children). My bear was named Thaddaeus (after one of the lesser-known apostles, sometimes called Jude), and I decided to knit him a lovely white sweater and crochet a blue hat. I suspect that many in the community thought I was involved in some kind of "backsliding behavior," but Thaddaeus proved to be very important when I left this community and found myself just south of the Scottish border in the city of Carlisle.

I was sitting on a bench just off a city street on an April afternoon. A big man in a torn jacket approached looking aggressive and put-out. "What are you doing?!" he asked me. "I am writing letters. With my friend Thaddaeus." Indeed, I was writing home, and my teddy bear happened to be placed on the top of my back-pack. Thaddaeus had on his lovely little sweater and hat. "I have a friend, too" the man said. He lifted his pants to reveal a knife strapped to his leg. The man said, "His name is Edgar."

In the old days, I probably would have begun thinking of the different ways in which "Edgar" would be used to kill me or, more likely, I would have started running. But on that day, I held out my teddy bear so that it was just a few inches from the knife and said, "Say hello to Edgar, Thaddaeus!" The man laughed.

Somehow that completely absurd, *ridiculous* encounter amounted to a sea change; it involved a very different sense of humor than my "encounters" with imaginary snow and so on. On the surface, nothing too dramatic happened immediately after-wards for Thaddaeus and me in the county of Cumbria in the city of Carlisle. The man and I had a beer in a nearby pub and we parted on good terms. The laughter was genuinely friendly and, to use biblical language, "without guile." I don't think the topic of religious faith even came up, but until that moment, as an adult, I would not have identified myself as a Christian.

All that occurred about thirty years ago, when I was the age of most of my current students. And while some things have changed for me, some things have not. I close with a brief account of an occurrence last year that involved a colleague, a surgeon's knife, and an owl—an occurrence that very much reminded me of the absurd but life-giving event involving Thaddaeus, Edgar, and recovery. Because this story involves *another* stuffed animal, I offer a brief defense of these sentimental objects in an endnote.

My colleague Ed faced a far more menacing and direct threat than I had faced in northern England. Ed had suffered a very serious heart attack in the fall. He had stopped breathing for at least two minutes until he was brought around by his wife, Lois, and a neighbor. He survived, and a bypass operation was scheduled for the winter.

Our department has a collection of owls in our lounge. The owl has been a symbol of patience, wisdom, and philosophy (the word "philosophy" comes from the Greek for "love of wisdom," and historically the symbols of philosophy and wisdom are often interwoven). To celebrate Ed's survival (so far) and to wish him a speedy recovery, my colleagues and I pitched in to buy a magnificent, brave-looking orange owl. The owl looked completely at home, nestled in between little statues of Socrates, Plato, and Aristotle. And yet our gesture, marking a man's recovery from a potentially fatal heart attack by getting him a bizarre but friendly stuffed bird, was not enough.

When it came time for Ed's operation, we noticed the owl was missing. We learned later that Ed had taken the owl to the hospital and placed it in the recovery room. He wanted to wake up looking at it. I can't think of a better way to wake up, once the mind-debilitating anesthetic drugs have worn off, than to laugh in front of an orange, feathery icon of wisdom.

Endnote: In Defense of Teddy Bears and Things Like Them

You may think teddy bears and toy owls are childish, but I think you would also be surprised how much good they and their makers do. Space only permits citing one case. Consider the author of probably the most sentimental tales *ever* written about animated animals: Beatrix Potter (1866–1943). Childish? Perhaps. But keep in mind that her stories were first penned to help a sick child; that she helped challenge some of the sexism of her day (the Linnaean Society would not let her present a paper at their meeting because she was a woman, but they also had to admit that her work on fungi was publishable); and that she bequeathed her very valuable farm property to the public through the National Trust. Lovers of Peter the Rabbit and teddy bears unite!

I Want to Hold Your Hand!

I ALWAYS THOUGHT GARDENS WERE SAFE. ALTHOUGH there was that incident in the Garden of Eden with Adam and Eve, the Serpent and the Fall, gardens generally have a good reputation. If you were to tell me that you always think of me as a garden, I would likely think of that as a compliment. It therefore felt like a cruel betrayal when I nearly died from a hand injury while gardening in Minneapolis this June.

I was wrestling with a honeysuckle tree when my right hand caught a huge splinter, something a surgeon would later refer to as "a foreign body." The wound triggered a menacing inflammation and infection, causing a steady wave of red to advance like an army up my right arm. The event turned—as probably many accidents do—from something that by itself seems trivial and insignificant into something huge and preposterously disastrous. The first physician I saw used a black pen to mark the "progress" of the inflammation. "If the infection goes beyond this line, I will hospitalize you." The infection went beyond the line. And yet the precise nature of the infection remained elusive, though the names of possible causes sounded like strange planets (e.g., streptococci, pseudomonas, enterococci). My hand seemed to have a life of its own. A nurse said, "Your hand looks very angry today." I don't like thinking of my hand as having an independent emotional life.

Nonetheless, I confess that the hand did begin to seem like a repulsive, foreign body itself.

As an academic I tried to maintain a certain detachment by studying major epidemic upheavals, especially (for some reason) that period of 200 BCE to 200 CE when the disease pools of four great civilized regions erupted: the Mediterranean, the Middle East, China, and India. Somehow this diminished my little "crisis" due to a honeysuckle tree, a crisis I was sharing with television personality Rosie O'Donnell, who was coping with a similar infection at the time. My studies also paved the way to be open to healing that surpassed all the technology of modern medicine. In his ground-breaking study of epidemics, *Plagues and Peoples,* William McNeill writes, "When all normal services break down, quite elementary nursing will greatly reduce mortality." In the end it was indeed *elementary nursing* that turned the tide.

Over two weeks Jil and a friend helped me dress the wound, holding my hand without disgust. More than a few nurses did the same before and after the surgery I finally had. The basic act of touching was overwhelming. It was as though the infection that had developed from a ridiculously small injury—which one physician came to describe as "potentially life threatening"—was being fought by the powerful yet also simple, and on the surface seemingly trivial, act of holding hands. I found some confirmation of McNeill's thesis in the chapter "Confluence of Civilized Disease Pools," where he recounts how plagues were combated by the simple Christian charity of touching and compassion.

McNeill's work (and my own experience) receives interesting support in one of the greatest epic poems ever written about a disaster that took place in a garden, *Paradise Lost.* In John Milton's epic poem, disease and death enter the world only when people *stop* holding hands. It is when Adam and Eve cease to hold hands that the Fall occurs (Book IX). The trauma happens when there is a physical and emotional distance, when instead of reaching to one another in love, each one in different ways grasps for power. After the Fall, it is only when Adam and Eve hold hands again (Book XII) that they find a hope for healing and redemption.

I Am So Sorry!

WHEN I AM WRONGED, I DESPERATELY HOPE FOR APOLOGIES, evidence of reform, maybe even, when appropriate, restitution. That, in any case, is the way I try to respond when I realize that I have wronged someone else. Apologies and evidence of reform (I cry) usually arrive with flowers. Once, after an especially regrettable dinner party, I sent elaborate bouquets of flowers to four or five people.

Sometimes, reconciliation takes its own course. I once forged a letter. I was a resident in a literary community in New Zealand (I have changed the nature of the institute, the place, and subsequent name to protect all parties but, alas, all other facts are true). In my defense, I can report that there were several other forged letters in circulation at the time that were designed to spark some romantic mischief, but these were all between good friends, whereas mine appeared out of the blue and was really, at the end of the day, utterly indefensible. When "Christy" discovered that I had forged a letter to her from "Patrick" she did *not* initially accept my apology. Later, she accidentally broke a wine glass at a party. Everyone heard the glass break but nobody saw it, thus enabling me to take the blame by shouting out, "I am so sorry!" As I was down on the ground by her feet cleaning up the spilled wine and broken glass, Christy looked down and said, "You are forgiven."

I suspect that we want and expect dramatic signs of regret

because we desire a sign of a radical break from the past. Or, more precisely, we want a kind of double movement: a sincere "ownership" or taking responsibility for the past harm (yes, I am the one who forged the letter) and yet at the same time a renunciation, a repudiation or dis-ownership. A contemporary English philosopher, Richard Swinburne, describes how a person who repents tries to "make the present 'he' in his attitude as different as possible from the past 'he' who did the act." When apologies seem too casual we simply doubt that any such double movement is under way. This is the likely reason why President Clinton's apology for the U.S. bombing of the Chinese Embassy in the Balkans a few years ago did more to add insult than repair damage. The problem was that the President made the apology standing before a golf course and wearing a golf shirt. We probably also want our apologies to be on the dramatic side because the wrongdoer is often unable to make full restitution. Restoring what was harmed would be ideal, but when that is not possible we are especially interested in evidence that the person does not in any way relish or regard the past harm as acceptable. Some of these elements come to the fore in two of Shakespeare's plays.

In *Macbeth*, Duncan, the King of Scotland, is traitorously killed by Macbeth. After the murder, Macbeth hesitates. There is a brief moment when he realizes the horror of what he has done and he wishes the deed could be undone or, more precisely, he wishes Duncan might rise from the dead.

> Macbeth: To know my deed, 'twere best not know myself.
> *Knock.*
> Wake Duncan with thy knocking! I would thou couldst!
> (Act II, Scene II)

It appears that Macbeth has a choice in this scene. He can confess, acknowledging the regicide and probably suffer a brutal punishment; but instead (with Lady Macbeth's help) he reconciles himself to what he has done. He develops what might be called a perverse integrity. Rather than reject the monster he became that night, he thoroughly wills that he, Macbeth, is indeed the person who did that savage act; there is no further effort to intentionally distance himself from the act through moral reform. As a result of uniting himself with (or failing to distance himself from) the murderer, Macbeth becomes less troubled when he plots and executes the murder of other people, including his friend Banquo. There are later signs in the play of a recalcitrant ambivalence or a kind of self-division that occurs in Macbeth's consciousness. As Gabrielle Taylor (a contemporary English philosopher) puts it, Macbeth moves from *being afraid for himself*—that is, afraid that he will be exposed as the killer—to *being afraid of himself*. Still, in the play Macbeth never returns to own and then disown his wrongdoing, and thus he dies unredeemed.

Shakespeare's *The Winter's Tale* offers more hope. Leontes, King of Sicilia, mistakenly believes his wife has been unfaithful with his good friend. After foiled attempts to poison his friend and kill his own daughter, he imprisons his wife, Hermione. Faced with his mad, public accusations, Hermione is reported to have died in despair. Leontes relents. He sees that what he has done is intolerable and mourns for sixteen years. The time of inconsolable, penitent grief is only broken when, unlike Duncan, Hermione returns to life. As it turns out, Hermione did not die, though her death is reported to the court and to us the audience. She has been in hiding. In the climax of the play, the king is led to see what he believes to be a statue of Hermione. The "sculptor" then awakens "the statue" and the king lovingly, penitently, gladly is brought together with his queen. The scene is remarkable for its poignancy. Here is the invocation by the "sculptor" for Hermione to live again; the drama is enlivened by the strong use of punctuation at the beginning.

Music, awake her: strike!   *[Music.]*
'Tis time; descend; be stone no more; approach;
Strike all that look upon with marvel. Come;
I'll fill your grave up; Stir; nay, come away;
Bequeath to death your numbness, for from him
Dear life redeems you—You perceive she stirs.

[Hermione comes down.]

Start not; her actions shall be holy, as
You hear my spell is lawful. Do not shun her
Until you see her die again, for then
You kill her double. Nay, present your hand.
When she was young, you woo'd her; now, in age,
Is she become the suitor?

Leontes [the king].   O, she's warm!
If this be magic, let it be an art
Lawful as eating.

(Act V, Scene III)

The jubilation at the end is due both to this re-generation as well as to the discovery that the king and queen's daughter lived and has fallen in love with the son of the man the king originally suspected of being unfaithful with Hermione.

This portrait of reconciliation is probably most at home in the Christian account of redemption, in which the resurrection plays a vital role. For on Christian grounds, one would need to look to a genuine miracle in which, say, Duncan and others *really are restored to life,* in order for us all to get to the point at which "dear life redeems." I take up this theme in a later essay ("The Passion and the Happiness of the Christ") but here I would like to connect the concept of forgiveness and reconciliation with one more element involving the emotions. I suggest that forgiveness and reconciliation ultimately (or ideally) involve the wrongdoer identifying with the one who has been harmed. There is a current romantic comedy, *Love Actually*, that gives a tiny glimpse of this.

In the film there is a married couple played by Alan Rickman and Emma Thompson. The Rickman character is unfaithful, and his wife confronts him. He says, "I've been a classic fool." She says, "You've made a fool of both of us." That seems right; his action has rendered their marriage absurd or pointless or possibly tragic. In *A Change of Climate* by Hilary Mantel, a woman reflects on her husband's infidelity. "It is in the nature of betrayal, she thought, that it not only changes the present, but that it reaches back with its dirty hands and changes the past." So how does one proceed from there? Well, if betrayal can reach back into the past, what about a restored fidelity?

Can love reach back its hands and change the past? Of course there can be no change in the facts about what took place, but the meaning or significance of those facts can shift. And they can begin shifting, I suggest, when the person who did the wrong realizes he did not just hurt her; he hurt them both. He put them both in a foolish position. The reconciliation between the Rickman and Thompson characters is not portrayed at length in the film. There is a scene of him returning from a trip; he kisses her; and he gives gifts to the children. The kiss is perfunctory, but in it, I think, lies the symbol of the completed act of reconciliation, the "I forgive you" or even "I accept your return" that is said in response to "I am so sorry!" and "I have returned."

John Bunyan (author of *Pilgrim's Progress*) once said that the gates of hell lie at the lips of redemption. He was probably reflecting on the story of Judas, who betrays Christ with a kiss. I do not deny Bunyan's phrase, but wish to extend it. If he is right, and the gates of hell are near the lips of redemption, then the reverse is also true. At the very gates of hell one may also find the lips of redemption, even if complete redemption involves many stages including confession, love, reform, maybe giving flowers, or picking up a broken glass at a party. Or even, ultimately, the resurrection of the dead.

The Rock of Gibraltar

THE ROMAN ORATOR CICERO, IN THE FIRST CENTURY
BCE, famously described a friend as a second self. This has always struck me as a bit odd. Presumably when you love your
friend you are not loving yourself (at least not directly), and
it would be strange if you thought of your friends as you or as
some kind of self-reflection. Probably my closest friend when
I was young could not have been more different from myself.
He was European, old (we met when he was in his sixties), and
retired from a lifetime of commerce. Despite our differences, or
maybe because of them, he became what he and I called "The
Rock of Gibraltar." That is, a key, strategic point of reference in
life, just as the Rock of Gibraltar has historically been a vital
political and economic reference point due to its crucial location
between the Mediterranean Sea and the Atlantic Ocean.

It was probably from Peter that I learned elementary things
about friendship. For instance: If you think a friend has said or
done something mean, please remember that your friend loves
you; talk things over. As St. Aelred of Rievaulx said, "Friendship
cannot exist without grace."

I learned other lessons as well. Keep your friendships in repair (a saying from Samuel Johnson). Friendship takes time;
space is needed in a friendship when events are not scripted or
shaped by "plans." Samuel Johnson explained that a friendship
is like a work of art. One cannot take in all there is to a painting

in one glance. Your eyes need time to get accustomed to the depth and scope of emotions in a painting, and something similar is true in encountering all great works of art—and the people we love most.

Peter also implicitly taught me the balance between attachment and detachment in friendship. Too much attachment and control can creep into even the most saintly souls. One of my favorite mystics, Hildegard of Bingen, was driven to very unsaintly action in her attachment to Richardis von Stade, a fellow nun, who eventually felt compelled to leave Hildegard's convent for another one. The problem (apparently) was a simple case of unwanted control, for when Richardis sought to leave Hildegard's monastery, the saint fell off the deep end with threats (Richardis managed to "escape" in the end). If Hildegard can get confused, look out!

Probably the most peculiar, surprising element I discovered in friendship with Peter and, eventually, with others, is that sometimes a conversation with a friend can feel as though it is occurring outside of time, or at least outside the time frame in which one usually lives. Lest this sound too mystical, let me rephrase it in terms of stepping back from all or most of one's tasks, and viewing one's life (or whatever) from a slight, almost playful, distance. No longer engaged in the battle or struggle at hand, one is able to enter a safe arena and look back on what is unfolding. A conversation with Peter could feel like magic. It is probably from those experiences of somehow stepping back into another time frame that I am very sympathetic with St. Aelred's thesis set forth in his twelfth-century masterpiece, *Spiritual Friendship:* true friendship does not end.

St. Aelred's dictum is not easy to unpack. Life is complicated. People move. If we cease being friends after you leave, was the "friendship" we had somehow false or imperfect? The Danish philosopher Søren Kierkegaard wrote of how some relationships

are interrupted and that sometimes one may wait for the return
of the beloved, much as a dancer might wait, poised to continue
with a dance once his partner returns. And just when does a
friendship end? This is not clear to me. When Peter died, did our
friendship end? I would say "no" whether or not there is an afterlife. But I think St. Aelred was getting at the point that if your
love of a friend is thoroughly tied to a specific event (whether
this be going to the same college or walking your dog) and it
ends when the event ends, there is the distinct possibility that
the true object of your love is the event. If you were principally
loving the person *during the event*, wouldn't you still care for the
person *after the event ended*? If Aelred is right, then to love a
person is to love someone who is more than any specific event;
indeed the love of another person, ideally, is not dependent on
the specific event. T. S. Eliot may have been onto this point when
he wrote, in *The Four Quartets*, "Love is most nearly itself when
here and there cease to matter."

In addition to the many meetings with Peter when I was
young, probably the most extraordinary recent moment I have
had in the experience of time and friendship occurred last summer when John, an English friend, was visiting. When he came
to our house after his grandfather's funeral we stayed up late at
night, drinking wine and looking over some of his grandfather's
personal effects. John's grandfather, an officer in the British Army
in World War I, was wounded in one of that war's costliest, most
tragic conflicts, the First Battle of the Somme, in July 1916. On
the first day, 20,000 British troops were killed; John's grandfather was among 40,000 troops who were wounded. John had
been given a little gray bag that bore a red cross and had in it a
few coins. I noticed a stain on the bag and, without thinking, I
smelled it. I knew it was blood. There we were in the year 2000
in winter, smelling a battle that had taken place eighty-four
years ago. It is not as though John and I engaged in any mystic

time travel or séance, or that we felt a bond with the grandfather as a brother. But it was clear that John and I do have deep love in our friendship, and I was able, in that moment, to mourn the loss of his grandfather (whom I never met) with the intensity one feels in mourning the loss of a friend.

During his illness, Peter told me, "When the Rock of Gibraltar sinks, the monkeys need to learn how to swim." The Rock of Gibraltar hosts a species of tailless monkeys called Barbary Macaques; they are the only free-living monkeys in Europe today. By "the monkeys," Peter was referring to me and other young men and women whom he befriended, many of whom he supported financially. His charitable giving was immense (up to hundreds of thousands of dollars annually). But we monkeys were able to be well, after he died, largely because of the lessons of friendship he taught. And maybe because of the fascinating impact that friendship with Peter had on my sense of time, I often expect to see him again around the next corner or in an airport or at my front door.

I think of Peter often (I have many of his books and letters to reread), but I especially thought of him when Jil and I were in England not long ago, visiting Runnymede meadows, where in 1215 King John signed the Magna Carta. Just off the meadows, in the woods, we came across an ancient oak tree, the oldest I have ever seen. Some people believe that the Magna Carta was signed beneath that tree. I mentioned to Jil, "This looks like a magic tree. Maybe this is where Merlin the wizard lives." I had not noticed that there was a man behind us. The man said, "He's just stepped out, actually." I thought: Exactly. Just like Peter. He just stepped out.

Hello Tiepolo

IN 1994 MY WIFE, JIL EVANS, APPLIED FOR AND RECEIVED A license to paint in Windsor Park in England, though the license did not grant her *carte blanche:* she was explicitly prohibited from painting any royals or royal carriages. Notwithstanding this stringent condition, being with Jil when she paints is one of my favorite occupations. The trick to painting in the park that summer was staying clear of pranks by our friend Andrew (not the prince), who would use a mirror to reflect the sun in our eyes whenever he wanted tea or more paint—one time causing a virtual stampede of deer in our direction.

Jil does not paint royalty or deer; she executes colorful abstract work based on observation of nature, inspired by the Italian painter Giovanni Battista Tiepolo. She is taken in by Tiepolo's huge ceiling paintings of intertwined beasts, clouds, angels, chariots, and gods. After returning from sketching Tiepolo paintings in a museum or a church, she is often ecstatic. This at least partly explains why, after a session with Tiepolo, Jil throws pillows, books, and whatever lies close at hand, up in the air, half-expecting them to float unsupported. In light of this I suppose it is no surprise that when we returned from England and got a dog this year through a Minneapolis breeder, he was named Tiepolo. Tiepolo is a lovely sheltie with a face that is divided in half, black on one side, white on the other.

Living with Tiepolo is like living with Tiepolo: I feel that

I am constantly in the presence of a celebrity. The dog has fans that any rock star would envy. He has brought whole villages here in the midwest of the United States to their knees as grown men and women turn into boys and girls, repeating lines like "Cute puppy!" or just "Wow." To date, he has brought five cars to a halt as strangers lean out of windows to ask about the dog. The last time, which occurred yesterday, nearly caused an accident that would have killed three people (including the author). The question "Where did he come from?" is sometimes asked in a way that opens the door to discussing the supernatural and or extraterrestrial. Some children in the neighborhood think of him as a mix of elf and angel.

Amid all the fanfare and magic, I have an uneasy feeling that Jil, Tiepolo, and I may compose the ultimate surrogate family. The dog treats us as canine stand-ins, and I suppose I sort of dote on him as one would a human child. We were coaxed into thinking this way through a dog obedience class here in Minneapolis. In a crowded room of dogs and human beings one of the "instructors" ordered, "All human persons, step aside."

Of course palling around with Tiepolo has its perks. Now that I am clear about the whole surrogate business, our god-children, nieces, and nephews can breathe a sigh of relief. Even my students may have lightened up. With gray hair and glasses, I am the age of most parents of my students, and while I think that acting in a paternal fashion with students is patronizing and should be avoided at almost all costs, every once in a while cases arise when a student expects a bit of approval from "someone of my parents' generation." This is fine, but it can sometimes lead me into thinking that graduation is the breakup of a family. One year, after a class of students graduated, I had to watch the movie *Goodbye Mr. Chips,* the older version, twice, to pull myself together. Forget Mr. Chips. Hello Tiepolo.

On the other hand, living with Tiepolo can be pretty humiliating. It takes time to adjust to being eclipsed by a dog. Sure, walking with Tiepolo provides an opportunity to meet "the beautiful people." In the end, however, it becomes obvious that these dazzling folks are not particularly keen on dropping everything to spend three minutes getting to know a forty-something academic. Sometimes I feel like the straight man for my dog's jokes.

Tiepolo loves almost everyone he meets. The mailman brings him treats. Neighborhood children ask to be photographed with him. (These requests are granted.) He initiated friendships with two neighborhood families. Tiepolo even helped me come to terms with my fear of huge dogs. When I was a boy I was attacked by a Rhodesian ridgeback, and this left me with a scar and the dreadful memory of being cornered in a small room for an afternoon. At only three months old, Tiepolo befriended a massive Rhodesian ridgeback. I still find it wonderfully unnerving to watch them play.

I am sure that our dog has faults. In the morning, when Tiepolo brings *The New York Times* in from the front door, he doesn't always bring it to Jil straight away. Though I have no first-hand experience of the relevant appetites and desires, I now believe that for some of us the temptation to chew newspaper must be overwhelming. But whatever Tiepolo's canine sins, he has helped me to tame my more arcane academic endeavors. Too often I have wound up being cornered by projects reminiscent of the intimidating Rhodesian ridgeback. Instead of living in a small room with such terrors, I now try to find a way to enter into one of Jil's paintings. I try to swirl along with Tiepolo's beasts, clouds, reflected light, and drapery, along with pillows and airborne books. And if in the midst of the soaring creatures and volumes of color our dog starts tugging on the curtains or herding deer in the wrong direction, there will be no scolding. I will more than likely join him in the romp.

The Knights of the Round Table
in the American Colonies

LAST SUMMER JIL AND I WERE SCHOLARS IN RESIDENCE (code for *tour guides*) in a colonial home just outside of Newport, Rhode Island, owned by the Colonial Dames. Built in 1728, it was the home of famous philosopher, clergyman, and natural scientist George Berkeley, his wife, and several companions. There were eccentric moments, such as when phone operators from India ("outsourced labor") called to confirm phone numbers and so on; they had a hard time understanding why there would be a society like the Colonial Dames. The society consists of women who trace their ancestors back to prominent figures in the American colonies. "Do you mean these women are actually proud of the time that America was a British colony?" I was asked. This seemed odd to the operator from New Delhi.

In preparing ourselves to become colonial residents we received strange advice from friends who thought we should branch out in our summer tour themes. "Why not include Arthurian elements like the legend of the Grail? Or maybe you could have a sword named Excalibur set in a rock in front and get kids to try to pull it out?" But when we got there, I actually did give some thought to Arthurian romance.

And I began to see that Berkeley had something fundamental in common with King Arthur and the Knights of the Round Table: They all failed. But not completely.

Berkeley came to the colonies to establish a base where he would raise funds, grow food, and attract students to begin a college in Bermuda. This was to be a theological college where students would train in the humanities, languages, and theology, and then return to the colonies. Bermuda at the time was considered very exotic; it was compared with the enchanted island where the wizard Prospero and his beautiful daughter Miranda lived, in Shakespeare's *The Tempest.* Berkeley's plan was ambitious and, had he succeeded, it may have had a very large cultural impact. (At the time there were only a handful of colleges in the colonies.)

The funds did not come and the plan was ultimately abandoned. One of the two children born in the almost three years the Berkeleys spent in Rhode Island died just before they could return to Britain. Most biographers of Berkeley consider his Rhode Island period a colossal failure.

The adventures of Arthur and the Knights of the Round Table have been told and retold; and the tradition is not over, as new books appear on Arthur and related figures like Merlin. In some respects the older stories represent the best of the medieval aim of restraining the violence of the nobility. Violence in Europe was sometimes checked by various campaigns such as the Peace of God and the Truce of God movements. Hand in glove with these efforts, there were also chivalric romances and *courtoisie* books aimed at teaching restraint and the codification of permissible force. Enshrined in these legends is the so-called Round Table Oath, to be taken at Pentecost by all the knights who pledge themselves to mercy and justice. But whether you read the Arthurian romances by Geoffrey of Monmouth or Chrétien de Troyes or Sir Thomas Malory, the stories of Arthur all end in disaster. There is the infidelity of Queen Guenevere and Lancelot. Lancelot kills Sir Gawain (one of my favorite knights). Arthur is mortally wounded in a battle with wicked Mordred, his own son.

But the failures in both cases were not absolute. Berkeley hosted students from Yale and visited both that institution (where he made a large gift of his books) and Harvard. One of the reasons why his dream of a college in Bermuda was never realized was that the British Crown (rightly) feared that the growth in education would in turn lead to a growing sense of cultural and political independence from Britain. In a sense, while Berkeley did not have his college in Bermuda, he had an impact on colonial culture *directly*, encouraging education and free inquiry in the oldest American colleges, rather than by way of the British island colony believed at the time to be midway between the New and Old World. Both the president of King's College (now Columbia University) and the president of the College of New Jersey (now Princeton) were followers of Berkeley. In tribute to his impact on American life, the city of Berkeley in California was named after him.

It may seem more difficult to see success for Arthur because, among other things, it is not clear that he even existed (though there is evidence from the historian Nennius in the ninth century of someone named Arthur winning the Battle of Mount Badon.) But there are at least two enduring themes from the Arthurian romance epics having to do with humility and equality.

Many of these epics underscore the need for humility; our greatest, most heroic, and most resolute knights and ladies falter in the pursuit of ideals, and thus all of us should be wary of hubris and vanity. This lesson is beautifully told in *Sir Gawain and the Green Knight* (1370), in which Sir Gawain, the youngest of King Arthur's knights, remains virtuous in most but not all trials. Sir Gawain breaks a vow by wrongfully accepting a silk girdle from a lady. It is in this tale that one most sees how adventures in the Arthurian tradition often involve errors of some kind. (One of the meanings of the word "error" is a roving excursion. A "Knight Errant" can be interpreted as a Knight who tends toward error.) Still, like Sir Gawain we are not to be overcome by our sense of guilt and shame, but to persevere in justice and mercy, and to do so with good humor. When Sir Gawain returns to Arthur's court he elects to wear the silk, green lace as a sign of his failure.

> "Look, my Lord," said Gawain, the lace in his hand.
> "This belt confirms the blame I bear. . . .
> For being caught by cowardice and courteousness."

But rather than ostracizing him, the court merrily welcomes him, donning similar silk lace as a sign that they, too, are fallen yet saved by grace. Just after Sir Gawain's public confession of sin,

> First the King, then all the court, comforted the knight,
> And all the lords and ladies belonging to the Table
> *Laughed at it loudly* [emphasis mine], and concluded
>   amiably
> That each brave man of the brotherhood should bear. . . .
> A band, obliquely about him, of bright green,
> Of the same hue as Sir Gawain's and for his sake wear it.

The ideal of equality is invoked by the image of the Round Table itself; it is an ideal related to Berkeley's dream of education and liberty. The Round Table is meant to symbolize parity, the recognition of one's peers. In the romantic tradition, this is understood to be sacred or willed by God. We often, I suppose, think of the table where Christ is believed to have celebrated the Last Supper with his disciples as rectangular, with Christ at the head of the table or, as with Da Vinci's famous painting, Christ in the middle, functioning as the leader. But there is also a tradition that the table Christ used in the Last Supper was round. This has been seen as a symbol of the enduring, sacred calling by Christ to equality and friendship.

In the tours, I did not try to link Camelot with the farm-house where Berkeley and his companions lived from 1728 to 1731. I knew that under the best of circumstances it was going to be a stretch; the farmhouse does not even have a table that is round. But if the question surfaced as to how Berkeley and King Arthur might be related, I was prepared to argue that, in their own ways, they both planted seeds that produced a harvest more important than the Vanderbilts' and the other powerful families whose social domination is valorized in the great mansions of Newport.

A Student's Tale

———•———

"I HAVE ABSOLUTELY NO IDEA WHAT I AM TALKING ABOUT.
Can someone help me?" The professor looked to us for assistance. One of her students volunteered a few suggestions, and
then another started to formulate a couple of interesting arguments. The professor looked relieved. "Now, *that* is what I was
trying to get at," she said. She was having a bad day, but was
saved by her students.

The occasion of students rescuing their professors is not a
dominant theme in literature, though it does crop up in one of
Charles Williams's poems. "Taliessin on the Death of Virgil" is
set in the next life. Virgil, the great Roman poet, has fallen from
the edge of the world. His students fly to his aid.

> Unborn pieties lived.
> Out of the infinity of time to that moment's infinity
> they lived, they rushed, they dived below him, they rose
> to close with his fall; all, while man is, that could
> live, and would, by his hexameters, found
> there the ground of their power, and their power's use.
> Others he saved; himself he could not save.
> In that hour they came; more and faster, they sped
> to their dead master; they sought him to save
> from the spectral grave and the endless falling,

who had heard, for their own instruction, the sound of
    his calling.
There was intervention, suspension, the net of their loves,
all their throng's songs:
Virgil, master and friend,
holy poet, priest, president of priests,
prince long since of all our energies' end,
deign to accept adoration, and what salvation
may reign here by us, deign of goodwill to endure,
in this net of obedient loves, doves of your cote and wings. . . .

I never did this for any of my professors, though I would have
liked to.

Probably the closest I came, as a student, to helping my professor involved Roderick Chisholm of Brown University. Chisholm
was, in my mind, formidable on all fronts. He was breathtakingly
brilliant. He was also quite formal; he rarely called me by my first
name and we never met in a social setting.

During my doctoral defense, I was asked a pressing, difficult
question. Chisholm came to my defense, answered the question,
and then added this comment to his colleague: "It's a good thing
you're not being examined today." The examination complete, I
drove home. I was surprised to find myself weeping the whole
way—not light and easy tears, but intense crying.

Why? I think it was because, after five years of working
with him, this was the first paternal or friendly kindness he had
shown me.

About twelve years later, I was able to offer a reply to his
kindness, though this did not involve soaring to his aid with
other students singing about a net of obedient love. There is a
series of books called *The Library of Living Philosophers,* in which
twelve or more critics offer an assessment of a living philosopher's
work, and then he or she is able to reply. The philosopher does

get the last word, but sometimes the criticism of one's life work can be quite grueling and unnerving. In the volume dedicated to him, Chisholm's critics were respectful, but they were still critics, and while Chisholm was able to answer most of them, ill health prevented him from replying to the final five critiques. I arranged with a journal to write an extensive review in which I replied to the last of these critics in the spirit of my teacher. Mrs. Chisholm read my review article to her husband. In a letter sent to me about two months before his death, Chisholm wrote that he hoped that some day I would have a student who would give me as much joy as I had given him.

Chisholm, and many of my best professors, taught me that the opportunity for reciprocation, for the giving and receiving of teaching, requires humility. I have a friend who likes to say this: "If you want to be illuminating, you must light yourself on fire." But I am convinced this is the wrong way to go. Professor Chisholm, Margaret Miles, Robert Nozick, and many other sterling professors were gentle souls, not the least bit self-involved or self-seeking. They opened for me a wider world of ideas and scholarship, and welcomed us into a great, capacious space. Lighting oneself on fire simply draws far too much attention to oneself.

Two ancient philosophers, very different from Chisholm and spectacularly bad at lighting themselves on fire, were Empedocles (495–434 BCE) and Peregrinus (second century CE). It is said that Empedocles jumped into the crater Etna to demonstrate his divinity. This inspired a compact poetic description of his ending:

Great Empedocles, that ardent soul
Lept into Etna, and was roasted whole.

Peregrinus sought to demonstrate his contempt for death when he cremated himself by leaping onto a massive fire at the end of the Olympic games in the year 165. But to learn the futility of such self-immolation, it isn't necessary to go to ancient texts. During class one day I accidentally tripped over a large coffee maker, leaving in my wake an expansive pool of coffee and a still-plugged-in electric cord that had somehow become stripped. When my foot landed on the cord, a rod of pain ran up my body, the lights flashed, and I went on my knees, creeping toward a window. *Not* very helpful from a pedagogical point of view.

Rather than my professors electrocuting themselves or jumping into craters and onto pyres, the best teachers I had were much more like Dante's mentor, Virgil, in *The Divine Comedy*. Dante and Virgil are separated by hundreds of years, yet Dante's study of Virgil earns him the privilege of being thought of as one of Virgil's students. (In Charles William's poem perhaps Dante is one of the students who comes to Virgil's rescue.) When Dante writes of Virgil leading him through the rocky, dangerous terrain of hell and then purgatory, Virgil is pictured as casting light behind him, not on himself or in front of him. The gesture helps Dante see what lies before him; it also enables Dante to judge for himself whether the road ahead is secure or whether a different path would be better. Virgil is depicted as serving or being underneath a greater light, the light of God that is revealed in the closing passages of *The Divine Comedy*.

The light that Chisholm and other teachers left me and other students is so precious because they did not direct it at themselves. In the company of these great thinkers one easily felt transported by ideas and themes, the passions that go beyond the boundaries of any single person's character. The early Christian theologian Origen pictured the afterlife as a school. To some, that might seem like hell, but thanks to Chisholm, Nozick, and the others, I see that as something to long for.

At one of the colleges at Oxford University all faculty are called "students." This practice is motivated by the conviction that all of us, however credentialed, remain students of something greater, be it our field of study or life itself. What I have been taught by Chisholm and others is that, at the end of the day, we are all students. They knew that they were not the great sources of light. They were there to use the light they were given to share with others.

Confessions of a Sleepwalker

———

LAST WEEKEND I LOCKED MYSELF OUT OF A ROOM IN A major hotel. I knew I did not have the key because I had almost no clothes on. I occasionally have the problem of sleepwalking, brought on by stress. Why can't we sometimes do constructive things when we sleepwalk, like execute a brilliant thirty-minute workout or compose a masterful orchestral opus? Regrettably, I was staying on the fourteenth floor of a downtown hotel in Philadelphia when I woke up outside of my room wearing just underwear and a watch. It was 2:30 A.M. I took the elevator down to the lobby. I prayed it would be deserted. To my horror, there were about a dozen people there. I had to wait in line at the front desk. I must have appeared to be a convincing sleepwalker (or, more likely, a huge embarrassment), as the person on duty gave me a key to the room with no questions asked.

For some reason, worry makes me prone to such zombie-like episodes. This last fall has been stressful for so many of my friends, who seem overworked and extra-worried, personally and politically and economically. It's as though we are strong on carrying out industrious work but weak on genuinely hoping that there is relief anywhere in sight. As a joke, at a friend's fiftieth birthday, I gave him the gift of a psychological test that he could take at leisure; it was advertised as a reliable guide to discovering one's pathologies. It was supposed to be funny, but when I gave it to him he stared at me with a kind of nervous hopelessness.

Lately I have taken refuge in repeated viewings of the second installment of *The Lord of the Rings,* called *The Two Towers.* I have been especially taken by the plea of Sam and Aragorn to have hope, even when things are most desperate. Hope seems to be a forgotten virtue today, even though it was once recognized as a central, prized ethical value along with faith and love. Hope, Faith, and Love are seen in Christian tradition as the three "theological virtues" which are to complement the four cardinal (sometimes called "pagan") virtues of practical wisdom (prudence), justice, courage, and temperance. Of course there are times when our lives can be practically hopeless, and hope seems like mere wish fulfillment. But for all of that, don't many of the real illnesses, absurdities, and tragedies we face seem far worse when we cease having a genuine hope for resolution and flourishing? I have a friend who has cancer. And yet she is a person of such resolute, courageous hope that her doctors must love her for that alone. I am increasingly convinced that the honest hope for peace, peace for ourselves and for others, personally and politically, is vital. A person who is without hope may still be brave, but she may also be more susceptible to forces that she believes will lead to inevitable disaster.

One unusual advocate of hope was the late British painter Francis Bacon. Perhaps because of his reputation for decadence an interviewer asked him, shortly before he died, what he thought of the afterlife. More specifically, he was asked whether he would prefer death to be a matter of complete oblivion or hell. Bacon replied that he would prefer hell. He said that yes, hell must be very, very bad, but at least there is hope of escape.

According to G. K. Chesterton, hope is principally a mature, sustaining virtue, one that develops over time.

It is currently said that hope goes with youth, and lends
to youth its wings of a butterfly; but I fancy that hope is
the last gift given to man, and the only gift not given to
youth. Youth is preeminently the period in which a man
can be lyric, fanatical, poetic; but youth is the period in
which a man can be hopeless. The end of every episode
is the end of the world. But the power of hoping through
everything, the knowledge that the soul survives its
adventures, that great inspiration comes to the middle-
aged; God has kept that good wine until now. It is from
the backs of the elderly gentlemen and ladies that the
wings of the butterfly should burst. There is nothing that
so mystifies the young as the consistent frivolity of the
old. They are in their second and clearer childhood, and
there is a meaning in the merriment of their eyes. They
have seen the end of the End of the World.

Obviously hope alone, even with merriment in the eyes, is not
enough. The next night in the hotel I did not merely hope that
I would not sleepwalk; in addition, I slept *fully clothed with a key
in each pocket*. Still, a wise, full hope for peace and goodness is
no mean thing. It can be a courageous refusal to despair. It can
be a declaration that rather than being controlled by fear of evil
and distress, one's allegiance and deepest loyalty are for goodness
and peace.

The Goblins and My Parents

PERHAPS WE SHOULD THINK OF TROUBLES THE WAY meteorologists think of storms. We should give them names. For example, why not say, "Here comes Ethel," rather than, "I need to adjust my medication again," or even, "Timothy has arrived," rather than, "The passive-aggressiveness of a professor is having a terrible impact on my morning"?

Lately, I have been dealing with "goblins." According to *Brewer's Dictionary of Phrase and Fable,* miners (long ago) attributed strange echoes in the mines to subterranean creatures they called goblins. Apparently the word *goblin* is related to the old German word for cobalt, a metal that miners regarded of no value in terms of wealth but as very dangerous. To me, a goblin stands for an event that is troubling and embarrassing, even if it is also sort of "funny," but not really.

Recent goblins in my experience include odd events in which I utterly fail. There was an academic conference last weekend in which the lecturer went on a rant. His language became increasingly abusive and insulting. His perspiration was copius. I was supposed to offer comments in reply. I thought to myself, "Maybe he just needs a hug." Wrong. Later on I completely misunderstood another speaker who was dramatically making the point that "we," the middle class, were now in charge of deciding whom to honor in our society. He said, "We are the ones who give the medals! We give the awards! We are the Medici!

We are the Fuggers!" He said the last word so quickly and loudly that I thought he said a similar word, with a substitution of "ck" for "gg." So I asked the speaker why he thought we were all Fu**ers. This event involved two goblins: first, the embarrassing fact that I would think the speaker would ever use profanity, and second, that I was "undereducated." Until that moment, I had not heard of the Fuggers, a prominent family of German bankers who thrived in the fifteenth century. I felt that I had somehow combined a lack of education and a prurient mind.

A really unfortunate goblin: Some friends were planning their wedding and asked me to find a passage on love. I proposed a passage from Nathaniel Hawthorne's correspondence with Sophia, whom he courted and married. One of the great lines in a letter from October 4, 1840, is as follows:

> We are but shadows—we are not endowed with real
> life, and all that seems most real about us is but the
> thinnest substance of a dream—till the heart is touched.
> That touch creates us—then we begin to be—thereby
> we are beings of reality, and inheritors of eternity.

My friends *loved* the passage and I introduced it at the wedding by highlighting the great love that Nathaniel and Sophia shared; I wished my friends that same, deep love. Upon getting back from the wedding there was a major article in the *New Yorker* (March 21, 2005) with the following title: "The Other Sister: Was Nathaniel Hawthorne a Cad?" Evidently, Nathaniel had a secret, and rather manipulative, love for Sophia's sister! The magazine featured a hideous cartoon of Nathaniel and Sophia holding hands and yet, with his other hand, Nathaniel is reaching out trying to touch Sophia's sister!

One last goblin: Last week I locked myself out of our house. Panic. My dog is inside! Nobody is around to let me in! The Key

Master is called! She unlocks the door! And then I look (again) in my pocket to discover I had a key all along.

My father had a stroke recently. This is no goblin, but a monstrous, sobering moment that puts to one side all upsetting moments at conferences and embarrassing times in class or with a Key Master. His condition has been stable since the stroke, but there has also been a certain lightness in my parents' tone and pace. Their days no longer pivot around accomplishments. Both of them said that, in the end, the most important thing in life is love. That language, so sentimental in so many contexts, carries serious weight when you are sitting with your parents around the kitchen table talking about health and the limitations of medicine.

I sometimes wonder whether the struggle with lesser evils like "goblins" should be seen as preparation for when the true disasters break in upon us. My pathetic time with keys and locked doors reminds me of a scene in *Pilgrim's Progress* that I now draw on in thinking about my parents. Three-fourths of the way through the book (its full title is *The Pilgrim's Progress from This World to That Which Is to Come*), Pilgrim and his friend Hopeful are captured by a giant named Despair and imprisoned in Doubting Castle. The giant's companion advises Despair to take the pilgrim and Hopeful and "show them the bones and skulls of those that thou hast already dispatched; and make them believe, ere a week comes to an end, thou wilt tear them in pieces as thou hast done for their fellows before them." In the morning, however, their fortunes are reversed.

> Now a little before it was day, good Christian [the name of the pilgrim], as one half amazed, brake out in this passionate speech: "What a fool," quoth he, "am I, thus to lie in a stinking dungeon when I may as well walk at liberty? I have a key in my bosom, called

Promise, that will (I am persuaded) open any lock in Doubting Castle." Then said Hopeful, "That's good news; good brother, pluck it out of thy bosom and try." Then Christian pulled it out of his bosom, and began to try at the dungeon door, whose bolt (as he turned the key) gave back, and the door flew open with ease, and Christian and Hopeful both came out. . . .

The night before their release Christian and Hopeful were beaten senseless by Despair. But for my part, I take heart with my parents. Perhaps, by God's grace, come morning there will be an escape.

Are We in a Crisis Yet?

"CONTROL YOUR DOG!" THE SECURITY GUARD SHOUTED as she burst into my office. My dog, Tiepolo, lifted his head momentarily and then resumed his nap. "I said CONTROL YOUR DOG!" she yelled. It was as though the guard had a gun (which she didn't) and had just stopped a criminal (which she hadn't) and gone through the routine of: Put your hands up. Step away from your car. And so on. She continued: "Remove your dog from campus now!" I was stunned. "I said NOW!"

A new animal policy dictates that Tiepolo not be on campus, despite the fact that he has been a much-loved companion who has attended nearly every class I have taught in the last four years. I understand the prohibition (a dog was involved in an "incident" a month earlier, thus forcing the college to adopt an official Service Animals Only policy), but I found the adrenalin that this "crisis" caused a bit unsettling.

Lately, there seem to be more crises than ever before. A year ago I found myself in several "crises" concerning administrative details. The issues were somewhat routine, even tedious; but several people responded with the concentrated, intense emotion and outrage that would normally be reserved for events like being locked out of your fallout shelter when a thermonuclear weapon is about to explode, or realizing that you and your family are the hosts of bubonic and pneumonic plague. Even casual social events have recently achieved the status of

57

unprecedented depth. A couple said they couldn't come for dinner because "Life has us by the throat." I imagine that was code for "We have a schedule conflict" or "I'm tired" or maybe even "I am still mad at my husband/wife/partner." But why should any such event evoke an image in which LIFE itself is assailing you? This encourages the thought that LIFE is a brutal, sociopathic murderer that routinely sets out to strangle innocent people with savage brutality in order to prevent them from attending dinner parties. I am not against a little hyperbole, but I worry that if you use up your most serious terms so that a social inconvenience is described in terms of *a brutal assault,* what language will be left when you are trying to describe an event in which *there actually is a brutal assault*?

St. Augustine once said that delight orders the soul. In a sense, I suppose this means that what you delight in will, in part, determine the state of your soul. For example, if you take great pleasure in cruelty, your soul is cruel. Augustine also spoke of the *ordo amoris,* or the order of love. Augustine was referring here to the way in which one's emotions are to fit properly the events at hand; seeing cruelty should arouse a concern for justice, seeing someone vulnerable should give rise to a desire to protect, and so on. In a sense, Augustine's view of values is similar to G. K. Chesterton's definition of sanity: Treat big things big, and small things small.

I have given examples of where I believe the "crisis" threshold is too low. One of the better literary portraits of the opposite problem is Flaubert's description of Frédéric Moreau in the middle of a riot in Paris.

> The drums beat the charge. Shrill cries arose, and
> shouts of triumph. The crowd surged backwards and
> forwards. Frédéric, caught between two dense masses,
> did not budge; in any case, he was fascinated and

enjoying himself tremendously. The wounded falling to the ground, the dead lying stretched out, did not look as if they were really wounded or dead. He felt as if he were watching a play.

I do not have a solution to finding the key to the right order of love. But I do have a feeling that the result of not finding this key or, worse, flaunting it, is disastrous. Let us agree that Frédéric is monstrous in his disengagement and lack of feeling. It is evident (I hope) that the state of his soul is not good. But I find it equally worrisome when we respond with extraordinary, excessive emotions (either positive or negative) to events that are either simply inconveniences or small charms. The problem at hand may relate to the darker side of sentimentality.

Oscar Wilde once said that "a sentimentalist is simply one who desires to have the luxury of an emotion without paying for it." I think he had in mind cases when a host of emotions (from ecstasy to a sense of great loss) are cultivated in contrived circumstances like a trite play or a manipulative, saccharin song, when in fact the emotions are not really warranted. In other words, when I cry to a sentimental song about loss, I may be doing something that is principally self-indulgent rather than really grieving a loss. Sentimentality can allow us to experience all sorts of emotions in a way that seems disconnected from the natural home for such emotions. Frédéric's problem was not sentimentality, but that (like the extreme sentimentalist) he was cut off from what was truly called for in his genuine crisis. Just as we would be responding inappropriately to something trivial (say someone falling asleep in or skipping our class) by acting as though the wounded are falling to the ground, the dead are everywhere, and our village is flowing with blood.

I am not rigorously anti-sentimental (see the essay "Drugs, a Bear, and an Owl: A Testimony"). I do suspect, though, that if we err with excessive, over-the-top emotions about comparatively trivial events we may succeed in thinking that our lives are very, very interesting, but simultaneously we may seriously dull our sensibilities when it comes to recognizing the truly outrageous. One example may suffice to bring this point home.

A few years ago the senior senator from Minnesota, Democrat Paul Wellstone, and members of his family and staff were killed in a tragic plane crash. There was a massive memorial service that included many Republicans as well as Democrats and Independents. At one point the service turned more into a political rally, and some of the Republicans either were, or at least thought they were, booed. Our governor (an Independent) left early and responded with anger. He said he felt raped.

Raped? While I have not been raped, I know too many people who have, people who have suffered the debilitating, long-term, profoundly scarring effects. The governor was not raped that evening, either metaphorically or literally. Just ask this question: Do you think any rape victim anywhere would ever say that their tragedy was like going to a funeral that turned into a political rally for a political opponent? To use the language of rape under the circumstances that unfolded at the memorial service is either to have a very diminished, damaged understanding of rape (a true crisis) or an inflated, almost delusional view of the "horror" of having Wellstone's son and close friends speak on behalf of the late senator's ideals.

By all means, let's enjoy a bit of melodrama, but in moderation and with reason, lest we lose the ability to recognize when we are facing a real crisis. There is a difference between being raped and listening to a peaceful political rally of a party that you disagree with, just as there is a difference between escorting off campus a four-year-old sheltie with a flawless record of friendliness, and facing down the dogs of war that Hernán Cortés unleashed in his massacre of the Aztecs in the early sixteenth century.

Going Down?
Several Problems with Hate

IN CLASS ONE DAY I ASKED, "WHY IS IT THAT A JOY SHARED is doubled, but a grief shared is halved?" Max, a brilliant student, looked puzzled. He pointed out that quite the opposite may occur. If you hate someone, you may feel quite happy when he grieves and if you learn that he has joy, this could even bring on a serious depression; it is painful to watch someone you hate having a good time. I realized: Max is probably right. I also wondered why Max should be such an expert on this topic.

My personal acquaintance with hatred is spotty, though I did go through a two-year patch of serious hatred I directed at one of my professors. I hated him so much that I killed him in an article I wrote that was published in a philosophy journal in Israel (*Philosophia* 1991). The paper is called "Imaginary Evil" and begins with a narrative in which I go to my professor's office and murder him. The paper then reads, "I have done other things in my dreams . . ." and takes on the topic of whether one can commit evil acts in dreams. Just before the paper went to press I changed the professor's name to one similar to mine, "Oliver" (my last name is pronounced "Toliver"), because I came to the conclusion that hatred of another person was killing me or, to be less melodramatic, it was harmful to me. The hatred I had was not a good kind. I did not even have the excuse that the characters had in George Orwell's classic *1984* when they were trained to hate others during daily sessions called Two Minutes Hate. My own two years of hate were built on juvenile resentment, insecurity, and, for lack of a better word, immaturity.

The kind of hatred that leads someone to delight in another person's grief has been called *malignant joy*. Malignant sorrow might be just as good a term for the condition of being pained by seeing someone flourish whom one hates. In an important study of moral emotions, the German philosopher Max Scheler (1874–1928) argued that this underlying form of hatred plays an essential role in resentment. In cases of resentment the one who hates is often powerless to annihilate the object of hatred; and it is because the hated object cannot be destroyed that the person finds "solace" in malignant emotions. Scheler pointed out that one of the problems of this sort of hatred is that a person can become defined by (and, in a sense, defiled by) that which he or she wishes to destroy. According to Scheler, when you hate something intensely, you (at least in the extreme) want to annihilate it. This may all be very well if you hate someone smoking or you hate theft; this hatred would simply amount to your wanting there to be no more smoking and robbery. But if you direct your hatred toward a person, things get dangerous.

One of the better examples of this soul-destroying hatred is in Victor Hugo's *Les Misérables*. A police inspector, M. Javert, spends much of his life hunting down Jean Valjean, whose initial "crime" (for which he served nineteen years in prison) was that he stole some bread to help his starving sister and her family. Javert is obsessed with Valjean; he is pained when any good fortune comes to Valjean, and he takes pleasure in Valjean's misery. In the end, Valjean dramatically saves Javert's life. Javert then faces a catastrophic plight. He takes Valjean into custody, but then realizes that he cannot successfully imprison him; he simply cannot bring himself to imprison a man who rescued his life. The meaning of Javert's life had become defined by his hatred of this man. Once he had Valjean in his power and could not bring himself to destroy his lifelong nemesis, his life lost all purpose. In the end, Javert kills himself.

Such poisonous hatred is the mirror opposite of love. Thomas Aquinas and others have understood love in terms of wanting the beloved to flourish; the lover naturally takes pleasure in the good of the beloved and grieves when the beloved is harmed. Just as hatred has a withering, annihilating effect, love has an affirming, generative effect. One can see this played out in many of Shakespeare's comedies, where hatred leads to infertility and self-enclosure, and proper romantic love leads to festivity and renewal.

But a puzzle remains. In fact, it was Max (my student Max, not Max Scheler) who went on to raise an important challenge.

Max argued as follows: Even if you truly love someone, why would sharing a grief with them halve or in any way reduce the grief? If you lost your brother in an accident and shared this news with your beloved, you might feel her affirmation of yourself, but your grief would be no less. Again, Max is probably right. But I suggest that while *the amount of grief* may be the same, there is a sense in which the love of another person may still reduce the grief, perhaps even reduce it by half. Consider Shakespeare's *Twelfth Night.*

At the outset of the play, two key characters are in a state of grief and despondency. Olivia's brother has died. She retires from the world and lives in almost continuous mourning. Orsino, the duke of Illyria, is in love with her, but because she rebuffs his overtures, he too is in a state of retired grief. The spell is finally broken by a brother-and-sister pair named Sebastian and Viola. Viola's philosophy is that none of us own ourselves completely; life lies in opening oneself to love, risk, and self-offering. After many scenes of disguise, a duel, a forged letter, and more, Olivia falls in love with Sebastian and Orsino falls in love with Viola. (This is a standard Shakespearean scheme in which all comedies end in marriage, and all tragedies end with funerals.) With her marriage to Sebastian, Olivia's grief over her brother's death may not be reduced (though the clown counsels her to be mindful that her brother's soul is in heaven), but as she throws off her self-enclosure and lets Sebastian into her life, she grows stronger.

Falling in love, in Shakespeare's world, is part of growing up, and it makes the bearing of grief easier even if the amount of grief remains the same; after all, a fifty-pound object is easier to lift when you are an adult than when you were a child despite the fact that its weight remains the same. The New Testament contains a brief maxim that speaks to this: "Love builds up" (1 Corinthians 8:1).

The malignant, immature hatred I had for my professor disappeared. There were many reasons it gave way, finally, to respect and concern; some of these are fairly commonplace, such as coming to appreciate his intellectual background and simply rereading and finding value in his work. And though I am a long distance from *loving* him, I have found an unexpected sense of kinship with him. As a professor myself I know that some day a student (I hope it will not be Max) might hate me so much that he or she will feel, and perhaps write, some of the bitter things I did once.

Love from Afar

THERE IS A MEDIEVAL, ROMANTIC TRADITION IN WHICH the lover courts the beloved from afar. The relationship usually is (supposed to be) chaste and poetic, and leads the lover to do heroic, chivalric deeds in honor of the beloved. Back in graduate school, my friend Chris had such a passionate and chaste love for Ann, yet Ann was marrying someone else. All Chris could do was to compose poetry he never sent to Ann and to reread *Sir Gawain and the Green Knight,* a fourteenth-century courtly romance. Chris tried to convince me that while there is what he called *the ecstasy of abandonment,* there was also *the ecstasy of restraint.* As a sign between Chris and me that he was maintaining ecstatic restraint, he wore a green tie at Ann's wedding to Robert. This green tie affair was a reference back to poor old Sir Gawain, a brave but not completely chaste knight; he kissed the lady of the castle and accepted a love token from her (not good), and though his life was spared, he ever after wore a green girdle as a sign of his failure to live up to his calling. As far as I know, neither Ann nor her husband has any idea why their wedding album features photographs of Chris with a green tie. Chris explained to me that he was engaged in *love from afar,* and that he would perform an anonymous yet heroic deed for Ann.

If you take into account cases when love does not attach to a person, love from afar probably happens all the time. My most recent love from afar was farming. It happened when I was team-teaching a class with a biologist, Professor Gene Bakko (whom *everyone* in my college community adores), combining agriculture and philosophy. For some reason I fell head over heels with farming, farms, and farmers. I was completely over the moon with Wendell Berry's portrait of rural, community life, the ways in which one's soul might be shaped by the seasons. Urban life seemed comparatively alienated from the earth and completely unconscious about our source of food and water. I did not try to conceal my new love; I told my wife, Jil, who was not very happy with the news.

I did not secretly treasure pictures of farmers, farm equipment, and crops; I did not slip away to look at tractors while I was supposed to be at a philosophy conference. But I did get into all kinds of trouble. Apart from looking into but ultimately deciding against buying a hobby farm (I had *no idea* farming involved so much work!), there was a disastrous conference at Michigan State University (an agriculture school) where I was invited to give a lecture on family farming.

The conference was sponsored by the National Science Foundation and brought farmers and those in the food transportation business together for talks by philosophers on a variety of themes: pollution, food distribution, water rights, the free market, and so on. The person who was to speak on family farms was ill, and so I was called in at the last minute. Under the spell of Professor Bakko, I wrote a paper that was published in an "Ag journal" on the importance of theological and philosophical literacy when thinking about agricultural policy. The director of the conference had no idea that my love of farming was kind of like Chris's love for Ann. Chris loved Ann from a distance; it was *romantic,* and not based on first-hand experience of the work involved in a sustained, real relationship with her. I tried to fit in with those who were attending the conference (flannel shirt and so on) but it soon became clear that I was out of my league. I started my presentation and used liberal quotations from actual farmers, but after about fifteen minutes I was interrupted by a rhetorical question: "You aren't a farmer, are you?"

I felt that I had been caught trespassing. Several minutes of painful silence followed and then someone in charge said something like, "Well, Charles, perhaps we should wrap this up soon." I did go on for about fifteen more awful minutes, but the only way I managed this was through unbridled, ruthless self-deprecation, and self-lacerating humiliation. My strategy was that if I succeeded in brutally attacking myself, the conference members would back off and not feel the need to hurt me. Comments afterwards ranged from "It was okay. Honest" to "Geez. You don't like yourself, do you?" Love from afar is not easy.

Many people love farming from afar, people such as the great Roman poet Virgil. His poem the *Georgics* (composed from 36 to 29 BCE) celebrates rural farm life with rhapsodic, almost ecstatic passages about trees, bees, and planting. But, as a colleague in classics puts it, there was simply too much copulation and defecation on the farm for Virgil who, basically, was more at home in Rome. (Of course, both those things went on in ancient Rome, too, so I have found this explanation a little thin.) In any case, Virgil was no farmer and his poem has, from time to time, been defended on the grounds that (as Seneca observed) Virgil wrote "not to instruct farmers, but to delight readers."

Never again will I try to offer a presentation on family farming at an Ag conference. And I am certainly not going to pretend to know anything deep from first-hand experience of disease control in crops, the corn belt, or irrigation. Be that as it may, I still hold a candle for farming and a growing appreciation for the immense work involved in agriculture. The next time I am at an Ag school or, better yet, on a real farm, I will wear a green tie and try to enjoy the ecstasy of restraint.

Conversations with Paintings

A NINETEENTH-CENTURY ROMANTIC POET ONCE SAID HE
would exchange the Alps in Europe for a single, good conversation. Fortunately nobody, to my knowledge, has ever been offered
such an exchange. Besides, the choice (mountains or conversation) may be open to question. I suppose it must be granted
that one cannot have an ordinary conversation with a system of
mountains that covers more than 80,000 square miles. But just
because something cannot speak in a conventional manner does
not mean one cannot have something like a conversation with
it. I am not sure about talking with mountains (where would
one begin?), but certain types of paintings are another matter. I
usually begin a conversation with a painting by saying hello and
asking something like, "How are you?"

Some paintings have a life of their own. Paintings themselves
(and not just the people portrayed, represented, or expressed in
them) can sometimes be happy or sad; they feel ecstasy, or agony,
or both; they can look wounded or malicious; vain or angry;
shy or boastful, and so on. Some painters, such as my wife, Jil
Evans, explicitly understand their works in terms of habitation
or dwelling. Jil sometimes talks of seeing a mind revealed in a
painting. By her lights, it is important to consider whether you
are seeing any of the following at work in a painting as a whole:
praise or blame, invitation or retirement, abandonment or restraint, eros or some other passion? Art criticism might well be

formulated in terms of whether the canvas as a whole offers an engaging mind-body relationship. Perhaps there is a profound and creative use of color and gesture so that the painting has an interior life, a life that is wise or foolhardy, clever or reckless. Jil's work has a layered psychology that I find enthralling. It is as though one can relate to her paintings the way one relates to another person. And sometimes it is the painting that begins the conversation.

There is an old Dominican monastery, now the Museum of San Marco, in Florence, where the paintings seem very much to have that intense personal presence. In some comments on the museum, Jil has said, "Some of these paintings are alive. And I don't mean that simply metaphorically." The work of Beato Angelico is everywhere in the cells of the different monks, depicting the resurrection, the passion, the annunciation, and other scenes from the life of Christ. To be in dialogue with any one of them would, I warrant, change one's soul. I believe these paintings are extraordinarily tender, gentle, and inviting; they coax the viewer into an exchange rather than command the viewer to do some act such as pray or repent or praise. Just looking at them (but I again warrant that these are paintings that are difficult to "just" look at) may already be to pray or repent or praise.

As a writer, I can do little more than offer testimony to the importance of conversations with paintings. I am unable to reproduce or display the conversation I had with Fra Angelico's *The Mocking of Christ*, with its beautiful use of red and green and shades of grey. Christ is being mocked by hands that are painted abstractly, and not attached to a body. The face that spits on Christ is also bodiless. The painting brought home to me something of the wholeness of Christ and the fragmentation of the forces that oppose the sacred—but just writing that (or reading it) sounds too thin and incomplete compared with the experiences one has in front of the painting itself.

At a conference recently put on by the American Philosophical Association, there were several presentations by prominent philosophers of religion, some of them Christian, some non-Christian. One philosopher was using a projector to display some notes. At the very end, all the notes were gone and there was simply a blank, white light projected on a screen. After the three hours of talk, I thought, "Wouldn't it be nice if someone were to step in and say, 'Let's take a different look at this topic, shall we? May I have the first slide of Fra Angelico's work?'"

Lady Wisdom

MY FIRST, AND SO FAR WORST, CASE OF PUBLIC SPEAKING happened in the tenth grade at an all-boys boarding school when I addressed about three hundred fellow students and faculty without a text. Public speaking looked so easy. What could possibly go wrong? David, a rival classmate (our English professor hung on his every word) gave a winning ten-minute address. Just before it was my turn, I thought it would be good for me to have a topic. I thought that *wisdom* was a great subject. One of my favorite Bible verses at the time was Proverbs 1:20, which in the King James Version reads, "Wisdom crieth without; she uttereth her voice in the streets." I began with these words: "Wisdom cries out in the street!" And then I added, "Let us listen to her." The next ten minutes of silence were painful. Rather than attribute this humiliating spectacle (though David said later that he thought the "talk" was "brilliant") to inexperience, some faculty suspected my poor performance (or, really, my failure to perform) was due to drug abuse. I was marched off to be inspected by the school nurse. Fortunately or unfortunately, I was not then, or before that moment, ever "on drugs." Drugs came later.

The image of Wisdom as a woman is replete in the Hebrew Bible/Christian Old Testament. Many centuries later Wisdom appears as a Lady in the work of the philosopher Boethius in the sixth century. The Lady is of only limited help to Boethius, alas, for she visits him in prison where, eventually, he will be executed by decapitation in the year 524 by Theodoric. In the meantime, however, Boethius and this sagacious Lady produce the classic *The Consolation of Philosophy*, a meditation on God's relationship to time.

One of the lessons of this work is that time as we experience it from moment to moment needs to be seen as only one level of reality. There is also eternity. Boethius thought of God as existing in an ideal unity; God's whole life is to be thought of as a moment outside of time. God is eternal, not caught up in the past and future. What to us is past and future is somehow present to God. In *The Consolation of Philosophy* Lady Wisdom gives us the following image of time and eternity.

> Eternity is the simultaneous and complete possession of infinite life. This will appear more clearly if we compare it with temporal things. All that lives under the conditions of time moves through the present from the past to the future; there is nothing set in time which can at one moment grasp the whole space of its lifetime. It cannot yet comprehend tomorrow; yesterday it has already lost. And in this life of to-day your life is no more than a changing, passing moment. . . . What we should rightly call eternal is that which grasps and possesses wholly and simultaneously the fullness of unending life, which lacks naught of the future, and has lost naught of the fleeting past; and such existence must be ever present in itself to control and aid itself, and also must keep present with itself the infinity of changing time.

This majestic, consoling portrait of eternity gave Boethius an overriding reference point, beyond the past, present, and what little time remained for him during his imprisonment. Yes, he would die soon, and yet he looked to a God who would aid and love him from the standpoint of eternity.

I am not sure whether Boethius is entirely right about God's relationship to time. I tend to think God is temporal or in time *now* without beginning and without end. But I also believe Lady Wisdom was on to something. This Lady, and Boethius, and also the author of the mystical work *The Cloud of Unknowing* each critique a life of passion that is limited to the *moment*. *The Cloud of Unknowing* teaches that "time was made for man, not man for time." We are not at our best when our current desires rule us and compel us toward immediate satisfaction. Perhaps most of us know (or we have "a friend" who knows) the unfortunate regret Shakespeare so aptly summarized as "Past reason hunted, and no sooner had;/ Past reason, hated . . ." (Sonnet 129). Boetheus' Lady Wisdom would probably reply that the problem here rests in a disastrous philosophy of love as well as time. Our loves should not be defined by time and fleeting moods or temporary passion. Probably the best critique of this blind passion is Denis de Rougemont's *Love in the Western World*, which argues that most of our Western literary celebrations of romantic passion end in death.

Rougemont begins his study with *The Romance of Tristan and Iseult*, the story of two lovers whose lives are cut short (inevitably) by death. The passion at the heart of their relationship involves a desire for endless happiness, which Rougemont argues must involve intolerable desire and suffering. "Every wish to experience happiness, to have it at one's beck and call—instead of being in a state of happiness, as though by grace—must instantly produce an intolerable sense of want." Though we today think of "passion" as life-affirming, buoyant, and vital, its original meaning was "suffering" (as in "the passion of Christ"). Rougemont contends that much of Western romantic tradition thrives on a kind of addiction to a passion that can never be fully consummated in life.

> Love and death, a fatal love—in these phrases is summed
> up, if not the whole of poetry, at least whatever is popu-
> lar, whatever is universally moving in European litera-
> ture, alike as regards the oldest legends and sweetest
> songs. Happy love has no history. Romance only comes
> into existence where love is fatal, frowned upon and
> doomed by life itself. What stirs lyrical poets to their
> finest flights is neither the delight of the senses nor
> the fruitful contentment of the settled couple; not the
> satisfaction of love, but its *passion*. And passion means
> suffering.

Perhaps Rougemont has overstated his case. And perhaps this
teaching is not exactly what Wisdom (whether appearing as a
lady or gentleman) would cry out today in the streets. But perhaps there is also something beautiful about a love that is not
caught up and defined by a history of passion. I had a slight taste
of this non-passion-driven, non-history-bound love recently.
The story is considerably less exciting than the love and death
of Tristan and Iseult.

A friend was in the hospital in New York City. On some
level I cared about her health and had even contributed some
money to help pay the medical bills, but for some reason or
other I had almost no *feeling* of care. Zero. Nothing. My mind
turned to a word of wisdom by the spiritual director Baron von
Hügel, who said something like: I kiss my child, not always
because I love my child but in order to love my child. When I
first came across this dictum, I thought that von Hügel must
be monstrous. What sort of parent would need to undertake a
strategy in order to cultivate the appropriate feelings toward his
son or daughter? But then I also wondered: What sort of person would feel no care at all when his friend is facing a medical
crisis? Perhaps both von Hügel and I are rather weak when it

comes to the natural flow of emotions. I thought: If von Hugel can kiss his child in order to love his child, maybe I can give my friend flowers in order to love her. The flowers worked; undertaking that simple act in a deliberate, somewhat detached manner opened me to a depth of affection for my friend. It was not the passionate desire valorized or lamented in Western lyric poetic tradition. But it was a steady, real, chaste affection that was somehow from a position not governed by passing moods or occasional sentiments.

The Wisdom tradition as it developed in Western Europe after Boethius sometimes speaks of virtuous love in terms of a paradoxical combination of heaviness and lightness. In the fourteenth-century masterpiece *Piers the Ploughman*, Lady Wisdom in the form of Holy Church tells us:

> Love is Heaven's sovereign remedy. . . . Heaven could
> not hold Love, it was so heavy in itself. But when it had
> eaten its fill of earth, and taken flesh and blood, then
> it was lighter than a leaf on a linden-tree, more subtle
> and piercing than the point of a needle. The strongest
> armour was not proof against it, the tallest ramparts
> could not keep it out.

I discovered in that hospital in New York City what I could have only guessed at as a boy giving an incoherent chapel talk. "Love is the physician in life," reports the Lady in *Piers the Ploughman*, "the power nearest to our Lord himself, and the direct way to Heaven."

Stay Awake

JOHN, AN ENGLISH FRIEND WHO TEACHES COLLEGE, RE-
ports that he actually fell asleep giving a lecture. It was after
lunch in a dark room when he was using an overhead projector.
He tells me that he doesn't recall falling asleep, but he certainly
remembers waking up. His afternoon sleep may have been a
very short nap as his students were still present when he woke
up. And for all John knows, perhaps all of them fell asleep for
a brief period. In any case, the incident reminds me of all the
biblical precepts about staying awake.

The scriptural dictum to stay awake is sometimes contextual-
ized, and the reason for staying awake is specified. For example,
being awake under certain conditions can help avoid embarrassment ("Blessed is he who stays awake and keeps his clothes with
him, so that he may not go naked and be shamefully exposed,"
Revelation 16:15, NIV) or avoid poverty and starvation ("Do not
love sleep or you will grow poor; / stay awake and you will have
food to spare," Proverbs 20:13, NIV). Christ admonishes his disciples to stay awake with him during his agony in the garden
at Gethsemane. Perhaps the widespread practice of vigils in
Christian tradition is in imitation of Christ.

I have participated in dignified, mature vigils, but I also participated in a less respectable event. One evening or, rather, at
1:00 A.M., a history professor and I thought it was a good idea
to phone a visiting French professor. In fluent French my friend

began: "We Catholics are staying awake, awaiting our Lord's return, while the Protestants sleep. Would you care to join us?" I am an Episcopalian, whereas my friend is Roman Catholic, but he assured me that in a vigil with Suzanne (the French professor) ecumenism would be essential. In any case, Suzanne (wisely) declined.

I suggest that the biblical precepts about staying awake amount to an injunction that one should live intentionally. Søren Kierkegaard compares two people who are employed to drive carriages. Both begin at the same town and reach the same destination. But one does this intentionally, guiding the horses with skill, while the other falls asleep and only makes it to the city by sheer luck. The difference between the two, according to Kierkegaard, is immense: the one who sleeps through the journey is really just a passenger and can't be said to be a carriage driver at all. Similarly, someone who simply lives without intention or direction is more of a *patient,* rather than a proper *subject* or *agent.*

It is interesting that in Shakespeare moral and spiritual regeneration is often depicted as a waking from sleep. This is very much in keeping with the biblical portrayal of regeneration and resurrection as an awakening (Psalm 17:15, John 11:11, Eph 5:14). Part of Shakespeare's genius, in my view, lies in his giving us a taste of what this awakening to a life of new intentions feels like, or even tastes like. One of my favorite Shakespearean cases of waking up occurs in *As You Like It.* Oliver was bent on the further torment of his younger brother Orlando. En route to capture his brother, he falls asleep in the forest. Orlando comes upon him in time to see a lion and a snake poised to kill Oliver. Orlando hesitates but eventually fights off the threat, though with cost—he is wounded. When he awakes, Oliver is overcome by his brother's mercy. They reconcile, and in the course of Oliver describing the event to another character in the play, he reports "from miserable slumber I awak'd." Oliver is then questioned. Isn't he, Oliver, the person who contrived to kill his brother? Oliver replies:

> 'Twas I, but 'tis not I: I do not shame
> To tell you what I was, since my conversion
> So sweetly tastes, being this thing I am.

(Act IV, Scene III)

His brother's love has raised Oliver to a new life. If Shakespeare is right, being awake tastes sweet.

Still Standing?

"I AM GOING TO LEVEL YOU. JUST LIKE THE TWIN TOWERS. You will not be left standing." This was said to me shortly before I presented a paper at a philosophy conference here in Minnesota in late September 2001. My topic was eighteenth-century Scottish philosophy. I was not expecting hostile debate, though I was focusing on what I thought was a racist line of reasoning in the thought of an Enlightenment hero, David Hume. While I didn't suspect that my critic was a racist, Enlightenment terrorist plotting my death, I wasn't braced for this exchange. I am from New York, and while I knew only one person who was killed in the attack on the World Trade Center, my cousin Frank worked there. It was only by chance or by grace that he was not in his office that day. Frank lost hundreds of friends and colleagues. At the philosophy conference, after my rival's remark, my breathing became shallow. I felt dizzy. I think my critic was trying to make a joke.

Finding the right kind of humor or pleasure was not easy just after September 11. I liked my mother's strategy. She and some friends meet regularly on Long Island, New York, for a reading group. They all knew people who had perished in the attack. There were memorial services, and everyone felt heart-rending grief. But early in the following December they decided to read the story of Christ turning water into wine. "We cannot forget joy," my mother remarked. She also told me that she brought a bottle of wine for the group. "We toasted to life and love and so on," she explained.

Since September 11, we continue to be surrounded by events that seem to dwarf our private lives. But apart from the action we can take as citizens or soldiers, I also think our personal interaction with one another on an everyday level may still be a vital point of reference in which we may show our humanity.

I attended a reading group in Minneapolis on September 12, 2001, where statements like these were flying around the room: "This book is ridiculous!" "Who picked the reading anyway?" The person who proposed the book (someone on break from NPR and who was tracking recent events) looked forlorn, shoulders sagging. Friends rallied to move the discussion to a better place. There was no changing of water into wine, and there was no heroism, but there was some tangible humanity in the effort to bring things round.

My mother is not a rescue worker, nor does she particularly like wine; she is an author of children's books (*In the Beginning*, among others). Still, her bringing wine to her reading group raised a smile.

I survived "the attack" by my critic at the conference, which turned out to be far less fierce than I feared. Still, I did need help recovering from his assault. I was aided by a very simple gesture. A bearded, spectacled philosopher hailed me in the hallway. I was feeling off kilter, but he was smiling, even laughing, when he said, "You are still standing."

Whether from a sense of relief or a sense of comradeship, my response felt natural and healing. I laughed.

PART TWO

Divine Love in Politics and Culture

The Counsel of the Wise

———•———

"TEACHING ETHICS" IS NOT EASY. MY FIRST ATTEMPT AT
this was in a community college that shared its campus with a
veterans' hospital. Periodically, veterans would wander into class
and simply stare at the students and me silently. During my
interview with the Dean we actually had to step over veterans
who had passed out or were sleeping on the floor. My class
consisted of thirty nurses who, if they earned a B or better, were
to have their classes paid for by their hospitals. When the Dean
observed, "This is not Harvard," I took it to be his way of saying
that I should make sure each student gets at least a B. I thought
that it would be great to begin class with a controversial topic.
Abortion seemed a subject that would fit the bill. I then planned
to make a smooth transition to suicide. As I introduced some
arguments for and against different views on abortion, the class
quickly became a shouting match. "You are a Nazi!" one nurse
accused another. "No! *You* are a Nazi!"

I do not think we did any ethics that day. Certainly ethical positions were shared—with enthusiasm—but I don't think
moral reflection begins until one weighs reasons for and against
one's own position. There are probably times when we should
not step back and academically speculate about values. To take
a revolting, hypothetical and extreme case, I presume that there
should not have to be lengthy discussion groups on whether
it is permissible to skin and salt innocent children. But in my

class and in the world at large I suspect that some stepping back and putting oneself in the other person's shoes is essential. Even in the extreme case just cited, there may have to be some detachment. If, say, society discovers an individual who has done the heinous act mentioned above, we as a society need to think through the parameters of responsibility. (Was the torturer fully cognitive of the wrong? Was he acting on impulses he could not control?)

I suggest that moral reflection often involves a mixture of attachment and detachment. We need to be attached to our experience of values, our history and traditions, but we also need to step back and put ourselves in the context of other histories and traditions. Clearly there is a danger of becoming too detached, too theoretical and removed from one's own experiences, but there is also a danger of excessive attachment in which one's own views are assumed (without argument) to be obvious and irrefutable. For me, in that veterans' hospital, the key was humor. I did not make up jokes about physician-assisted suicide, for example, but I did seek to encourage a light touch in our discussions. At first this was largely unplanned; my first "joke"—or, better, our first moment of laughter—was when I accidentally fell off my chair. There was also the humiliating event when I was making a point about the danger of hypocrisy and the importance of clear language. I misspelled the word "hypocrisy" on the blackboard. I wish this had been on purpose.

Of course there should be only limited recourse to farce in serious moral reflection. I can't imagine the United Nations would have composed a better Declaration of Human Rights if the deliberations had been interspersed with good physical humor or stand-up. Still, some of the best moralists of the past were also good humorists. This was true of Erasmus, and especially true of his friend Thomas More. Both men were distinguished by their profoundly deep moral and religious convictions. And yet both combined humor, play, and satire with their Christian humanism and plea for tolerance and nonviolence. Erasmus' *Praise of Folly* is a masterpiece of frivolity and irony, followed by an earnest, moving defense of ideals. More's life was marked by jesting and jokes alongside the convictions about moral integrity that led to his execution in 1535. Even when he was about to be beheaded he jested with the executioner. "See me safe up," he said to the person helping him climb up to the scaffold. "And for my coming down let me shift for myself."

Moving Images

OFTEN IT SEEMS THAT OUR DEEPEST THINKING INVOLVES images. We probably don't so much carry around millions of beliefs about the world as we carry around a series of images or pictures of ourselves, friends and family, nation and religion, planet and outer space. Sometimes these images seem frustratingly stagnant. In teaching college I often find myself simply fleshing out alternative images of what is already familiar to a student or of what a student assumes to be domesticated. So, students sometimes believe the ancient Greek philosopher Socrates was, except for his dramatic execution, tediously academic. There is an another view of Socrates, however—veteran of a defeated army. Understood in the context of a fierce war in which Socrates had a reputation for bravery, the image of Socrates challenging the "wisdom" of Athens becomes more vivid and immediate. I love the way one colleague tries to break through to a student who has a dour, fixed view of some subject. For example, when a student once complained that he did not like Japanese, my friend said, "Well, maybe Japanese doesn't like you." The student later confessed that he had not thought that studying Japanese was studying something *alive.* (I should add that my friend uses different techniques and images to cajole students; I don't think he ever suggested to a student with failing grades that she or he was not liked by World History or by entire disciplines like Mathematics.)

There is currently a philosophy of imagination that I find extremely limited. On this view, when you imagine something, whatever it may be—a house or a peace conference or a monster—there is nothing in what you imagine that you did not place there yourself. You cannot simply imagine a nondescript monster and then be shocked by discovering that it is vegetarian. After all, you are its creator, so you are the one with the responsibility of specifying what kinds of things your monster eats. There may be some limited truth to this account, especially when it comes to certain kinds of narratives—for example, "Once upon a time, a group of monsters used their fiery breath to create whole fields of popcorn. . . ." As the author of this scene, I did not exactly creep up on my monsters (or images of them) and describe them like a journalist or historian. I created them. But this view of authorship, imagination, and images seems far too narrow and domestic to me.

A case for the dynamic role of images can be made in almost any area, but I will stick with a controversial, central case: Religion. Consider any of the images at the heart of the great world religions: the exodus of the people of Israel from Egypt (Judaism); the passion, death, and resurrection of Christ (Christianity); the revelation of Krishna to Arjuna as described in the Bhagavad Gita (Hinduism); and the Buddha receiving enlightenment by a Bo tree (Buddhism). While Islam resists images of Allah, surely the language in the Qur'an and in prayers draws on images of compassion, mercy, and justice. These various images have lives of their own. Consider only the Hindu portrait of Arjuna and Krishna.

In the holy book the Bhagavad Gita (the "Song of the Lord"), there is a war. One of the greatest warriors, Arjuna, is disheartened. Before the battle commences, he has an extended dialogue with his charioteer, who turns out to be Krishna, the Lord God of all. Krishna teaches Arjuna about the nature of the soul, the meaning of life, duty, wisdom, and the divine. Arjuna learns of God's omnipresence and the importance of devoting himself to truth and to his vocation. His vocation is to be regarded as itself sacred. The image and teaching of the divine Krishna and his warrior pupil have many layers. On one level it may appear to valorize war, but on another level all the imagery of war and battle may be seen as metaphors for strife and conflict. Gandhi, one of the greatest advocates of nonviolence, for example, saw the Bhagavad Gita as his key inspiration. Part of the beauty of this holy book is the way it moves, opening up different pathways and vistas depending upon when and who is reading it. The text is alive. Part of what the text does (for me) is to compel a much-needed partial retreat from the desire to succeed in whatever task I am undertaking. Krishna admonishes Arjuna to abandon attempts to control all the outcomes of his action; so much happens in life that we simply cannot control. As T. S. Eliot interprets this teaching of Krishna, "Do not think of the fruit of action" (*Four Quartets*, "The Dry Salvages"). This advice and the imagery of Krishna and Arjuna have (I believe) a power that goes beyond descriptive prose:

> Arjuna: Krishna the changeless
> Halt my chariot
> There where the warriors,
> Bold for the battle,
> Face their foemen.
> Between the armies
> There let me see them,
> The men I must fight with,
> Gathered together
> Now at the bidding
> Of him their leader,
> Blind Dhritarashtra's

Evil offspring:
Such are my foes
In the war that is coming.

Sanjaya (to Dhritarashtra): Then Krishna, subduer of
the senses, thus requested by Arjuna, the conqueror of
sloth, drove that most splendid of chariots into a place
between the two armies, confronting Bhisma, Drona
and all those other rulers of the earth. And he said:
'O Prince, behold the assembled Kurus!'
     Then the prince looked on the array, and in both
armies he recognized fathers and grandfathers, teachers,
uncles, sons, brothers, and many other familiar faces.

The dialogue that follows moves with extraordinary imagery of the
soul, life and death, pain and pleasure, passion and illumination.
     One of the most inspiring, overwhelming sections of the
"Song of the Lord" is Krishna's revelation of his divine reality
(IX–XV). This appeal in Hinduism (as well as other religions)
to how the reality of God in the end surpasses the power of
our language to describe it may raise a warning light. Once we
go "beyond language," are we in a realm of pure superstition
and nonsense? We might be, and speaking as a philosopher I
strongly suggest that we always accept our fallibility; you and
I may practice a religion, and do so with devotion, and yet we may
be wrong. But it is equally important, I suggest, to appreciate
that reality may well extend beyond our best language, images,
and science. G. K. Chesterton once complained about those
who always demand linguistic proof for religious belief, and the
same complaint probably applies to religious disbelief:

Whenever a man says to another, "Prove your case;
defend your faith," he is assuming the infallibility of

language: that is to say, he is assuming that a man has
a word for every reality in earth, or heaven, or hell. He
knows that there are in the soul tints more bewildering,
more numberless and more nameless, than the colours
of an autumn forest. . . . Yet he seriously believes that
these things can every one of them, in all their tones
and semi-tones, in all their blends and unions, be accu-
rately represented by an arbitrary system of grunts and
squeals. He believes that an ordinary civilized stock-
broker can really produce out of his own inside, noises
which denote all the mysteries of memory and all the
agonies of desire. . . . For the truth is, that language is
not a scientific thing at all, but wholly an artistic thing,
a thing invented by hunters, and killers, and such artists,
long before science was dreamed of.

If Chesterton is right, we should be prepared to acknowledge the
possibility of realities (sacred or profane) stretching out beyond
language, and perhaps images as well. But at the same time, we
should not, I think, treat religious language and images as hollow
and fruitless. They can, instead, be vehicles that take us to deeper
and deeper realities. Following Chesterton, I suggest that inquiry into religious belief, languages and images is not a scientific
undertaking; it is more of an artistic exploration of art, a creative
investigation of creativity or a wise search for wisdom.

An exploration, I believe, of the great world religions involves becoming aware of how these religions become bear-
ers of a living wisdom. Such exploration also, I think, involves
asking which (if any) of these living traditions truly discloses
some reality behind it or through the images. A friend tells
me he is more interested in *questions* about religion, the world,
and meaning, than in *answers*, but I suggest that the deepest of
questions about life (from "What, if anything, is the meaning of

life?" to "Is there a God?" to "Is the Buddha's view of suffering emancipatory?" to "What is the soul?" and so on) only have a hold on us to the extent that we think one or more of them may truly disclose what reality is. If I became completely convinced that no deep truths were available through any of the religions, I would naturally also ask whether there was any point to asking questions in the context of these religions. When Gandhi recounts in his powerful autobiography how he was led to a life of radical nonviolence he continually stresses the centrality of truth in the service of God, so much so that he writes, "I worship God as Truth only." I read this as Gandhi's expressed allegiance and search for God as beginning and ending in an uncompromising desire to see and respond to reality as it is. Lest it seem arrogant for someone to seek truth (or Truth) in the great world religions, it is useful to take into account Gandhi's insistence upon rigorous humility.

> The instruments for the quest of truth are as simple as they are difficult. They may appear quite impossible to an arrogant person, and quite possible to an innocent child. The seeker after truth should be humbler than the dust. . . . Only then, and not until then, will he have a glimpse of truth. The dialogue between Vasistha and Vishvamitra make this abundantly clear. Christianity and Islam also amply bear this out.

The search to find which moving images in which religions seem the deepest and most disclosive can be enriching in ways that are unpredictable. If indeed these sacred images have a life of their own, that is exactly what should be expected. But one thing I found in my case is that by entering a single religion one can actually deepen one's appreciation and love of other religions. As a Christian, I believe some things (e.g., Jesus Christ is God incarnate) that are not accepted by Jewish and Muslim friends, but I believe endless things in common (beginning with the belief in a good Creator) with them. More important for Christians than comparing "beliefs" is to know a little of what it means to be called to revere the sacred and to meditate; to recognize the likeness of spiritual practices and use that recognition to forge a fruitful bond between people of different faiths. In graduate school in philosophy, none of my classmates explicitly professed a religion except for one Buddhist. While he and I had different beliefs about the soul, God, and Christ, we had a similar way (or a similar ideal) of practicing meditation, cultivating compassion, seeking to put aside acquisitions and self-possession, and so on. Even if one believes Christ is wholly human and wholly divine *(totus deum)*, it does not follow that Christ is the whole of the divine *(totum dei)* or that the divine cannot be authentically encountered in other religions or secular contexts.

I suggest that when the great world religions are in conflict or foment violence (internal to the institutions or externally), this is a result of the central religion's images hardening into projections of hate, much like my earlier narrative of monsters. How else can one explain how Christianity, as a religion, can move from the loving, tender, but demanding teaching by Christ in the New Testament, toward images in which Christ is used to oppress and persecute others? When religions calcify around hateful, violent ends, their images (however beautiful to begin with) become life-denying traps. The result is akin to Denis de Rougemont's concise critique of passionate lust in the classic *Love in the Western World*. Such lust involved a kind of "denuding intensity; verily, a bitter destitution, the *impoverishment* of the mind being emptied of all diversity, an obsession of the imagination of a single image."

Be Nice!

———•———

THERE IS CURRENTLY A TELEVISION BROADCAST OF PO-
litical debate ("Crossfire") that seems defined by the number of
times one party interrupts the other. And in between the inter-
ruptions you usually find *extraordinary* accusations hurled by the
speakers at one another as well as at a host of public figures. If even
half of the accusations turn out to be legitimate, probably everyone on the show and hundreds of politicians should stand trial
for treason, fraudulence, embezzlement, and more. I believe the
debaters think the performance is entertaining or amusing. The
"Presidential Debates" in 2000 and 2004 were also rancorous, full
of accusations, sneers, and so on. I was more than a little worried
that in one of the Bush v. Gore debates, when they were standing
fairly close together, one or both of them might "get physical."

My worry over all this may appear to be a concern about
"politeness." Isn't "politeness" a fairly light virtue when it comes
to politics? Why be polite when debating abortion, war in the
Middle East, or the integrity of a campaign? Politeness doesn't
seem to hold its own against powerful vices. For example, there
have been historical situations in which polite people have done
horrific acts. Some of those in charge of concentration camps
in the Second World War were supposedly cultured and loved
classical music and poetry. In both ancient and contemporary
culture, politeness seems to be almost completely irrelevant.

Consider the most vivid case from ancient history, in which

there was a mixture of politeness and political and military in-
timidation. During the Peloponnesian War, the Athenians con-
fronted the neutral island of Melos. The Athenians demanded
that the people of Melos join in their fight against Sparta or
face annihilation. The Athenians based their policy on "the good
of our own empire." On a certain level, however, the exchange
between the Athenians and Melians was extraordinarily polite,
with nobody interrupting anyone else. The historian Thucydides
offers the following transcript of the exchange. The Melians
calmly object to the Athenian policy of encroachment.

> [The Council of the Melians replied to the Athenians:]
> No one can object to each of us putting forward our
> own views in a calm atmosphere. That is perfectly rea-
> sonable. What is scarcely consistent with such a pro-
> posal is the present threat, indeed the certainty of your
> making war on us. We see that you have come prepared
> to judge the argument yourselves, and that the likely
> end of it all will be either war, if we prove that we are
> in the right, and so refuse to surrender, or else slavery.
>
> Athenians: If you are going to spend the time in
> enumerating your suspicions about the future, or if
> you have met here for any other reason except to look
> the facts in the face and on the basis of these facts to
> consider how you can save your city from destruction,
> there is no point in our going on with this discussion.
> If, however, you will do as we suggest, then we will
> speak on.
>
> Melians: It is natural and understandable that
> people who are placed as we are should have recourse
> to all kinds of arguments and different points of view.
> However, you are right in saying that we are met
> together here to discuss the safety of our country and,

if you will have it so, the discussion shall proceed on the lines that you have laid down.

Admittedly, what took place afterwards was not polite. Here is Thucydides' account:

> Siege operations [by the Athenians] were now carried on vigorously and, as there was also some treachery from inside, the Melians surrendered unconditionally to the Athenians, who put to death all the men of military age whom they took, and sold the women and children as slaves. Melos itself they took over for themselves, sending out later a colony of 500 men.

But it could be argued that, until the siege, everyone seemed perfectly well behaved. The philosopher Thomas Hobbes was one of the first English translators of Thucydides' history of the war between Athens and Sparta and, perhaps in light of the superficial propriety of the Athenians in the dialogue, he called politeness and cordiality "small morals," traits not worthy of being considered *real* morality capable of *real* justice.

Granted we should not treat politeness as itself a cardinal virtue, but perhaps, as G. K. Chesterton suggests, politeness and cordiality are the shadows cast by the great virtues. Whether or not there is true politeness often hinges upon whether there is a true, vigorous grounding in the big virtues. After all, while the Athenians did not interrupt the Melians and they patiently entered into dialogue with them, they were not really being polite and cordial. It is not polite to threaten people with annihilation. The "politeness" of the Athenians was simply a thin mask and not at all a reflection of true respect. Their behavior is akin to hypocrisy, which simulates virtue (there is an old saying: Hypocrisy is the compliment that vice pays to virtue) but does no

more than that. And, going back to the commanders of concentration camps, when I read about how this or that kommandant
liked good poetry while at the same time overseeing genocide, it
makes me even more revolted (if that were possible) than before.
How is it that a person can like the poetry of Goethe and yet be
a mass murderer? I have to conclude that such a person is particularly perverse—capable of understanding the feelings of others but nonetheless deliberately refusing to exercise that power,
settling instead to order the sociopathic, mechanistic destruction
of fellow human beings as though they were some disease.

The call for people to be polite to one another is not likely to
rally huge support (mass rallies, fundraising, etc), and I do not
know anyone who thinks that any major evil event in the world
was the result of anyone being impolite. My point is somewhat
different: Look at cases where civility breaks down, and let us
consider why. I suggest that our political gestures and debates
be polite because politeness reflects a deep understanding of
the value and dignity of each person. Our frequent failure to be
polite may not, by itself, be grave, but it may still be a sign of
something profoundly disturbing. In the late Republic of Rome,
debate in the Senate ceased being polite. Caesar hired people
to heckle speakers and, occasionally, there were even cases of
throwing manure at targeted senators. The lack of politeness
was not some awkward, momentary rudeness. It was a sign that
Caesar wanted supreme power and that the days of the Republic
were quickly coming to an end.

Rather than imitate the crude rudeness of screaming television
commentators, I propose that we consider the exchange between
Mercy and Truth in the allegory told in *Piers the Ploughman*.
Represented by two ladies who meet under dire circumstances,
they do not always talk with serenity, and yet they do reach concord in the end.

The account of their meeting is majestic:

Mercy was her name, and she seemed a very gentle lady, courteous and kind in all that she said. And then I saw her sister come walking quietly out of the East, and gazing intently westwards. She was very fair, and her name was Truth; for she possessed a heavenly power that made her fearless.

The Ladies Mercy and Truth do not agree on all the issues and some of their exchanges seem quite sharply edged. At one point, Truth shouts: "Hold your tongue, Mercy, and stop talking nonsense!" (They are discussing claims about Jesus' resurrection.) But with the help of another allegorical figure, Peace (who comes dressed as Patience), they are, in the end, nice to each other. So nice, in fact, that all three make the following proclamation about peace:

> There was never a war in this world, nor wickedness
>   so cruel,
> That Love, if he liked, might not turn to laughter,
> And Peace, through Patience, put an end to its perils

But Deliver Us from Evil

IN THEIR 2001 THANKSGIVING LETTER TO THE NATION, the First Family recalled the disasters we had been through that fall. The Bushes went on to highlight the great good that we had witnessed: bravery, charity, and compassion in the response of so many to 9/11. I believe that it is fitting for us to give thanks for all such noble, life-enhancing acts. But I also think it important, especially when thinking about September 11 from a religious point of view, to be clear about the difference between two kinds of good. Although the point may seem didactic or too obvious for a holiday letter, I wish the Bushes had noted the difference between the *good of justification* and the *good of redemption*. The first kind of good is used to justify evil, and is familiar to anyone who adopts an ethic in which the end justifies the means. To understand redemptive good, one has to step back a bit.

In the early days after September 11, prominent American theologians were asked why God allowed this horror to happen. Jerry Falwell speculated at first that the attack may have been justified due to our nation's sins. Fortunately, this was a minority view. Why did so many other theologians respond that this tragedy is in some respects a mystery? I suspect that the answer lies in the following proposition: To believe in an all-good, all-powerful, all-knowing God is not the same thing as believing that everything that happens is justified or good. A key component of Judaism and Christianity is that God does no evil. Islam also holds this. "Allah does not wrong people at all; people wrong themselves" (Qur'an, Sura 10). When we act with cruelty, things happen that God hates; such cruelty should not take place.

When we human beings do terrible things to each other, why doesn't God intervene? Perhaps God *should* annihilate any creation that has a certain magnitude of evil and start over. Actually, some theologians think that is precisely what God should do with the cosmos. This theme is replete in much of Shakespeare; *Hamlet, The Merchant of Venice,* and other plays make the point that if we demand *only* justice, none of us would survive.

From a theological (and Shakespearean) point of view, the only thing preventing this is the possibility of redemption and mercy. Consider an analogy involving a case that George Bush may have encountered as a governor.

Someone committed crimes which, in some states, merit the death penalty. Imagine that the criminal reforms, repents, desires to make whatever restitution is humanly possible and, where human aid must end and only a God can help, she seeks God's help in making things right. From a legal and moral point of view, perhaps the person *should* be executed. But from a religious perspective that gives center stage to redemption, this is a case that should involve pardon and mercy. Imagine the person is pardoned and goes on to do great good. None of that good ever justifies the crimes or makes them less brutal. Still, some good has come out of a wrongful past.

The three great monotheistic religions believe something similar about God. Rather than God destroying a creation gone wrong, Judaism, Christianity, and Islam hold that God works to bring great good through the terror and horror of our world. Unjustified wrongdoing can be the occasion for these redemptive goods, acts of unmerited mercy, compassion, and courageous love. Our term *redemption* comes from the Latin words for restoring and freeing; in gaining or regaining the goods of compassion, courage, and the like, we may come to have profound moral and religious integrity. Redemptive goods do not, however, *justify* or *lessen* the evil that occurred. Consider another analogy involving relationships.

Imagine you betray a friend, and the friendship mends gradually over time with renewed love. It may be that you now have a deeper, more profound friendship than if the betrayal had never occurred. You have loved your friend and been loved by her through thick and thin. The relationship has been regained or redeemed. Imagine the relationship has grown in scope and depth. Still, the betrayal was unjustified and should not have occurred.

When thinking about our national disaster of September 11 from a religious point of view, I believe it is vital to emphasize a central feature of redemption: the subsequent great good the Bushes point to is about the redemption of people or the nation, not the redemption of the event itself. Honoring the dead and the subsequent bravery and compassion shown by so many are ways in which we display a greatness of soul. Our national character may be refined and profoundly deepened through recent events in contrast to the way in which peacetime might, by comparison, leave us callously self-centered. But whatever great good comes about, this does not turn something evil into something good. The terrorist act of September 11 remains evil (and thus, contra Falwell, unjustified) no matter how much good happens subsequently.

Are there some people who are unredeemable? Perhaps. It is hard to picture Osama bin Laden and the leaders of al Qaeda repenting, showing grief for past wrongs, and it is even harder to imagine what any terrorist might do to make amends. Have there been events, whether on September 11 or at other times, which are so awful that no substantial redemption of any kind is possible? Secular and religious views may diverge here. If you believe there is a God of love who has limitless, infinite power, you believe that God has resources, overt and covert, that far surpass our wildest imagination. While religions of redemption diverge in their teaching about just how much of creation gets redeemed, they are united in the belief that the ills of this world do not have the last word.

William Thomas Cummings (1903–1945) once said, "There are no atheists in the foxholes." I strongly suspect that if you are in a foxhole and hope there is a God, you are not interested in justification. You don't want to be convinced that everything going on around you is happening just as it should. You are probably quite convinced that something has gone horribly wrong. I believe that hoping in God when you are in a foxhole is hoping that there will be victory or peace or that your friend who was killed yesterday is in heaven or that you will survive the night ahead.

In short, people in foxholes long for redemption, not justification.

Prayer and Foreign Policy

GEORGE W. BUSH IS NOT THE FIRST REPUBLICAN WHO champMioned free trade, was successful in an Ohio election, and was reputed to be a man of prayer as well as accused of fostering United States imperialism.

Under the leadership of the twenty-fifth president, William McKinley, the United States went to war with Spain following the sinking of the U.S. battleship *Maine* in Havana, despite the fact that Spain declared itself ready to make substantial concessions in restitution (even though Spain was probably not responsible for the explosion). The media at the time portrayed the Spanish policies in Cuba as brutally repressive, and McKinley thought it was our Christian duty to defeat the Spanish (which the U.S. did) in Cuba, the Philippines, and at sea. In settling on the terms of peace that were eventually determined in the Treaty of Paris (1898), McKinley considered prayerfully whether the United States should take possession of the Philippines. McKinley later told a group of clergy:

> I walked the floor of the White House night after night until midnight; and I am not ashamed to tell you, gentlemen, that I went down on my knees and prayed Almighty God for light and guidance more than one night. And one night late it came to me this way—I don't know how it was, but it came—(1) that we could

not give them [the Philippines] back to Spain—that would be cowardly and dishonorable; (2) that we could not turn them over to France and Germany—our commercial rivals in the Orient—that would be bad business and discreditable; (3) that we could not leave them to themselves—they were unfit for self-government— and they would soon have anarchy and misrule there worse than Spain's was; and (4) that there was nothing left for us but to take them all, and to educate the Filipinos, and uplift and Christianize them, and by God's grace do the very best we could by them, as our fellow-men for whom Christ also died. And then I went to bed and went to sleep and slept soundly.

McKinley, like Bush, believed that both in going to war and in the subsequent settlement he was following God's will. "The march of events rules and overrules human action," McKinley declared. "We cannot be unmindful that without any design on our part the war has brought us new responsibilities and duties which we must meet and discharge as becomes a great nation whose growth and career from the beginning the Ruler of Nations has plainly written the high command and pledge of civilization."

As a Christian, I think it is good for our leaders to pray and to think in terms of our responsibility as a nation to care for others. I worry, however, as many did in the late nineteenth century, whether "prayer" and "faith" may mask self-interest and national ambition. McKinley's faith, like Bush's, may well have been sincere and heartfelt, but there was and continues to be danger when faith and patriotism unite to dull the importance of self-questioning and inhibit the consistent pursuit of justice. Before highlighting the Christian tradition of linking prayer with a healthy, rigorous practice of self-questioning, consider

some other parallels between the military occupation of Iraq
and the Philippines.

McKinley thought that the case for military action against
Spain should earn widespread international approval, but this
was not in the offing. The United States military achieved early,
substantial success. When the U.S., along with some Filipino
fighters, defeated major Spanish forces, independence from
Spain was declared (still celebrated in the Philippines on June
12). Spokesmen for the U.S. military announced that they came
not as invaders or as conquerors, but as friends. McKinley's
policy was education and democracy in the Philippines, and
this was at first welcomed by the people. But when it became
apparent that this policy was linked to the Philippines being
under U.S. sovereignty, Filipino leaders felt betrayed and the
people rose in revolt. It took two years of counterinsurgent
violence before there was appeasement. This bloody conflict
was called by the United States a matter of insurgent violence,
while the people of the Philippines called it the Philippine-
American War.

The criticism of U.S. policy in the Philippines, like the policy
in Iraq today, is also somewhat parallel insofar as both sets of
critics point out apparent inconsistencies. Just as critics of Bush
initiating war with Iraq point out apparent inconsistencies with
our not going to war with North Korea (which has Weapons
of Mass Destruction), "liberals" in the 1890s like Moorfield
Storey protested apparent inconsistencies between our allowing
independence to Cuba but not the Philippines. "Why," asked
Storey, "should Cuba with 1,600,000 people have a right to
freedom and self-government and the 8,000,000 people who
dwell in the Philippines be denied the same right?" Critics at
the time suspected that the true reasons behind the occupation
of the Philippines was due to its dramatic political, economic,
and military advantages for projecting U.S. power in the Pacific.

In historical perspective, it appears that the nineteenth-century critics had a point.

In Christian tradition there is an important strand of self-questioning and of reverent toleration of others. In the modern era, we find this in Blaise Pascal (1623–1662), in the Cambridge Platonists who preached tolerance and nonviolence in the seventeenth-century English Civil War, and in Søren Kierkegaard (1813–1855), among many others. These Christians were keenly aware of the power of self-deception, and the ways in which self-interest can be ushered in under the banner of piety. These Christians counsel prayer that comes from a spirituality that is not presumptuous, that involves rigorous questioning of when our true motives slip from justice to narrow self-interest, and when our confidence that we are doing God's will is (tragically) wide of the mark. The outcome of the Spanish-American War teaches us the dangers of an uncritical mixture of prayer, spirituality, and foreign policy.

Dying on Campaign

—·—

"U.S. SEN. PAUL WELLSTONE, THE FIERY, FIST-SHAKING liberal fighting for a third term, was killed Friday morning [October 25, 2002] along with his wife and daughter and five others when his twin-engine plane, groping through snow and fog, crashed into a bog while landing in northeastern Minnesota" *(St. Paul Pioneer Press)*. The death of Paul Wellstone, his wife, daughter, and their companions is a profound tragedy deserving our deepest grief and remorse. There is also something else that is deserved.

There is a tradition, pagan at first but also Jewish and Christian, of military virtue on the field of battle. The glory of a soldier is not always in his or her survival of a war, of dying old by the fireside in the company of a faithful dog. There is glory in a soldier dying bathed in the blood of his wounds, fighting for the life of his people. You can see this in the oldest poem in the West, Homer's *Iliad,* or in the epic, medieval poem *The Song of Roland,* where the Christian warrior, Roland, dies fighting against overwhelming odds. The Hebrew Bible has the narrative of David beating Goliath, but it also has Samson dying in his final struggle against an occupying force.

The death of the people around Paul Wellstone makes no sense in relation to this tradition, but I find something substantive in it when it comes to the senator: Wellstone saw himself as a fighter. While his health was not optimal, he was in some

respects at the height of his political power. He achieved a reputation of being "the conscience of the Senate." He had just cast
an important, dramatic vote against war with Iraq, securing a
voice of opposition in the Senate. His first and last act on the
national stage as our senator was solitary and courageous, and
bore the sure, distinguishing marks of conscience and integrity.
He died on campaign, fighting for ideals of fairness, justice, and
the restraint of military power. While his aim was decidedly
political and pacific, he does share in the glory of a fighter who
dies in battle for what he believes to be a just cause.

Consider one of the earliest historical accounts of a soldier's
death in the West: the Battle of Thermopylae in the fifth century
BCE. Leonidas, a Greek commander and the Spartan king, held
a narrow pass with three hundred Spartan soldiers against repeated assaults by a massive invading Persian army. Leonidas and
his soldiers perished, but their bravery inspired Sparta, Athens,
and their allies to successfully repel the Persian onslaught. It is
recorded that at one point the Spartans were told that they had
no alternative but to surrender, for the Persian arrows would be
so plentiful that they would block the sun. Dianeces, a Spartan
soldier acclaimed for his bravery, is said to have replied, "All
to the good . . . if the Persians hide the sun, the battle will be
in shade rather than sunlight" (Herodotus, *Histories* 7.226). The
Spartans' death was later marked with an inscription by the poet
Simonides, recorded by Herodotus (7.228) as:

Stranger, tell the people of Lacedaemon
That we who lie here obeyed their commands.

There are some glories which should not be sought. It would
have been better, in my view, if Leonidas had survived, and I
wish with all my heart that the tragedy of October 25 had not
occurred. We all know, too, that the tradition of finding glory in

heroic self-sacrifice can be horribly misplaced. The old dictum of the Roman poet Horace (65–8 BCE) about love and death— "Lovely and honorable it is to die for one's country" (*Dulce et decorum est pro patria mort*)—has been ill-used to cover up the dehumanizing nature of modern warfare. Witness, for example, the hollowness of Horace's precept in *All Quiet on the Western Front* by Erich Maria Remarque. But while the notion that courageous self-sacrifice for one's country is a glory that can be abused, it can and should also have a proper place in a just struggle. And in Wellstone's case the concept of finding glory through courageous struggle was in his fighting to the death precisely to avoid the horrors that Remarque displayed in the book and were later rendered in the 1930 film. There is a glory, I suggest, in Paul Wellstone's fight to the end, his defiance against great opposing strength. He was true unto death and this fidelity deserves our praise and emulation. Through our grief over his death and the death of his companions, the fidelity of our senator should inspire us to take the ideals for which he fought even more seriously and bravely.

The Romance of Politics

SINCE SEPTEMBER 11, I HAVE SOUGHT CONSOLATION IN literature. I began by reading Augustine's fifth-century masterpiece *The City of God*, which testifies to God's providence notwithstanding the relentless battering the Roman Empire received from the Visigoths. A few months later, when the "War on Terror" got serious in Afghanistan, I was completely at home in Tolkien's trilogy *The Lord of the Rings*, with its stark contrast of good and evil. Now, with the collapse of Enron and the Justice Department going after various CEOs, I have been spending time in Dante's fourteenth-century dramatic poem of the afterlife, *The Divine Comedy*. I have been especially interested in Dante's intimate portrait of hell.

At the outset, there was one key question I took with me as I followed Dante though the *Inferno:* Which circle of hell would the Enron executives occupy? Dante mapped out three major circles: the incontinent (filled with those who did not control their desires), the violent (against self and others), and the fraudulent. Dante did not hesitate to locate specific people, contemporary as well as ancient, in various quarters, and so I thought my approach to his masterpiece was in keeping with the spirit of its author. Finding executives from Enron or the odd employee of WorldCom is not always easy, however. If you go straight to the realm of the fraudulent you will see as many as ten ditches, each designated for a different kind of fraud. If your executive acted out of pure greed, that would put him or her in one of these ditches, but more specific forms of avarice (nepotism, for example) require special treatment.

Unfortunately, after a great deal of initial enthusiasm, I must confess that my tour of hell became quite unsettling. First, there was the predictable problem of finding characters in the *Inferno* who resembled oneself. A vain old teacher, Brunetto Latini, in the seventh circle of hell, looked somewhat uncomfortably familiar. But second, and more importantly, Dante's view of hell prevented me from any kind of relish in contemplating the fate of CEOs in the *Inferno*. Dante does not work from a hatred of injustice. I feel sure he would be as outraged as you or I upon learning that three of Enron's top executives were awarded a total of over 56 million dollars in 2001 when the company was on the verge of losing $1.3 billion, leaving thousands destitute. But Dante would condemn whatever wrongdoing comes to light because of his love for justice and goodness, not his loathing of injustice and evil. The center of gravity for Dante is the love of political justice.

Dante depicts his own journey through hell to purgatory and then to paradise as his journey to a divine political justice. I was surprised by how much talk there was of politics in Dante's heaven. Today, the word "politics" gets bad press. Recently our President referred disdainfully to some congressional action as "a matter of politics." Our former Governor here in Minnesota once condemned legislators by calling them "political." Why this use of the term? Dante recommends a vocabulary that is refreshingly different from that of Mr. Bush or Mr. Ventura. Politics is a high, heavenly, loving calling. The affairs of hell are not worthy of being called *politics*. Hell is a perversion of politics, a twisting or breaking of something that should be good and wholesome. Heaven is political. It is a place where the common good is lovingly upheld, and individuals are recognized as worthy of attention, respect, and affection. From heaven's point of view, the perfection of a political community is a good, mutually supportive concord.

Augustine offers some theological insights about world history, and Tolkien is hard to beat when it comes to an all-out battle between good and evil. But when we think about setting things right after Enron, I think Dante should be our guide. Dante would want to see justice done, and for him that would mean that punishment, if it must come, after careful, fair-minded inquiry, should flow from our love of the good, not our hatred of evil. The difference between these motives can be quite significant. Imagine that you have a choice between two equally skillful surgeons save one difference: one chose to be a physician because she loved health, and the other because she hated illness. I would choose the first. A physician can always get rid of sickness by getting rid of the patient. Love of health, like love of justice, should be the starting point, not disdain for disease and wrongdoing.

At the pinnacle of Dante's poetic journey in paradise there is a consummate blend of politics and romantic love. Dante's beloved, Beatrice, directs Dante toward the justice of heaven. In the midst of his love for Beatrice, Dante falls in love with political justice. What makes hell, hell, is that it sins against the romance—the genuine, deep attractiveness—of justice. By tracing the mature desire for justice in *The Divine Comedy,* I came to agree with Dorothy Sayers, one of Dante's translators: Limiting your study to Dante's hell makes you run the risk of thinking that you can see the city of Paris by only studying its sewer. We run a similar danger if we subordinate our love of justice to our hatred of injustice.

From Russia with
Faith, Hope, and Love

I HADN'T PREPARED FOR ALL THE KISSING. I WAS PART OF a delegation of Anglo-American philosophers in Moscow in June 2001. Assembled by a scholar from Oxford University at the invitation of the Metropolitan Filaret of the Russian Orthodox Church, eight of us were lodged at a conference center adjacent to the Danilov Monastery in Moscow, the residence of our host, His Holiness Alexy II, Patriarch of Moscow and all Russia. Over four days there were two welcoming addresses, sixteen lectures, and a final wrap-up session. I was struck by the high quality of scholarly reflection, the depth of religious sensitivity, and, not least, the customary greetings. In the presence of His Eminence Filaret, a senior figure in the Orthodox church, monks, priests, and laity would sometimes touch the ground, then kiss his hand, and, finally, kiss his beard. Nuns would greet each other with two to three kisses.

Russia became Christianized gradually, with the Christian faith achieving a central place in the culture in the tenth century under Grand Prince Vladimir of Novgorod. As in Western Europe, the Church's history is often profoundly interwoven with social, political, and military upheaval. The ruthlessness of the twentieth century, not only for the Church but also for all of Russia and the U.S.S.R. as a whole, is difficult to imagine. Stalin's execution of priests and persecution of Christians are well known now, as are his insidious, more wide-ranging campaigns. What is now sometimes called Stalin's Terror Famine in the Ukraine, from 1932 to 1933, may have killed up to seven million people. The Great Purge of 1936 to 1938 involved 600,000 executions. In the 1930s the prison and labor camps had 1.5 million prisoners; by the 1950s this had increased to 2.5 million. No wonder that during our conference, an old priest stood up in a moment of silence and said the history of the Church in Russia is a history of crucifixion.

Our topic was the doctrine of the Trinity. This may seem completely abstruse and have nothing whatever to do with practical moral concerns, political or otherwise. But the reality of the doctrine and how it was articulated seemed increasingly vital to me, for it had to do with affirming, in the Godhead, the reality of three persons (Father, Son, Holy Spirit) who are yet united in nature as one God. Kallistos Ware, Bishop of Diokleia, one of the British delegates, said, "'United yet not confused, distinct yet not divided': such are the divine persons, and such also, although on a different level, are the human persons-in-relationship who are formed in God's image." Bishop Ware and several others upheld the Trinity as an icon or symbol of fulfilling, rich human interaction. "God is self-giving, solidarity, reciprocity, response . . . God is shared love, not self-love: such also is the human person." The portrait of the Trinity was everywhere. It seemed to symbolize a deep, profound unity that respected differences. It also suggested a longing for unity as well. Rather than the tumultuous, often violent political efforts at flattening out differences between people or compelling undesirable unions, the doctrine of the Trinity stood out as a serene concord of persons and nature. In this light, it was moving to witness so many Russian Orthodox Christians reverently kissing Rublev's famous icon of the Trinity.

All the kissing reminded me of one of the most poignant

scenes in Russian literature, a conversion. At the end of Leo Tolstoy's *The Death of Ivan Ilych,* the main character, Ivan, is on his death bed. He has lived a self-absorbed life, in an unhappy marriage, and yet in the end he struggles toward the light.

> Ivan Ilych . . . caught sight of the light, and it was re-vealed to him that though his life had not been what it should have been, this could still be rectified. He asked himself, "What is the right thing" and grew still, listen-ing. Then he felt that someone was kissing his hand. He opened his eyes, looked at his son, and felt sorry for him. His wife came up to him and he glanced at her. She was gazing at him open-mouthed, with undried tears on her nose and cheek and a despairing look on her face. . . .

This moment, when Ivan looks with love on his son and wife, is a radical breakthrough.

> And suddenly it grew clear to him that what had been oppressing him and would not leave him was all drop-ping away at once from two sides, from ten sides, and from all sides. . . . He sought his former accustomed fear of death and did not find it. "Where is it? What death?" There was no fear because there was no death. In place of death, there was light. . . .

The end of the novel involves a complete reversal; Ivan thinks at first he is falling into darkness, whereas he comes to realize he is rising toward light.

There was some tension at the conference. All the phi-losophers and theologians were male except for an American, Eleonore Stump. While Russian culture has occasionally been progressive in advancing the role of women (women were given complete civil liberties by the Provisional Government in 1917, though this was withdrawn when the Bolsheviks seized power), the vast weight of Russian history has been oriented otherwise, and the Russian Orthodox Church will probably be the last Christian institution to ordain women as priests.

At the outset, Eleonore expressed her unease about the under-representation of women. Still, this point of criticism was put aside as the week progressed, and Eleonore was the first of our delegation to speak in the wrap-up session of her deep sense of gratitude to our Russian hosts. I was very moved by the way Eleonore was recognized in this concluding discussion by His Eminence Filaret of Minsk and Slutsk, the Patriarchal Exarch of all Belarus, and the Chairman of the Synodal Theological Commission.

"Eleonore. With love, you are given the floor," he said.

I could have kissed his beard.

Heaven in China

OVER THE PAST FIVE YEARS I HAVE BEEN PART OF DIF-
ferent philosophical delegations to the People's Republic of
China, visiting two universities in Beijing and offering a course
at Hong Kong Baptist University. I was nervous in making my
first trip, having studied some of the more brutal periods of
repression in Chinese history, such as the Qin dynasty in the
middle third century BCE. The Qin only lasted fourteen years,
but I was unnerved by the fact that, in their effort to consoli-
date power, they not only burned all books contrary to their
thought—they actually buried, alive, scholars and their students
who had memorized texts that did not fit into the Legalism (a
contemporary term for the Qin teaching). I mentioned this to
a professor of Chinese history at my college. He replied, straight-
faced, "But the scholars were not alive for very long." This did
not calm my nerves.

The Chinese scholars and students I met were all exceptional
hosts. There was a great hunger for discussion, especially on
such topics as the philosophy of religion, politics, and econom-
ics. In Hong Kong, people conveyed a keen sense of the loss of
democratic life since the city and the surrounding territory had
returned to Chinese sovereignty. Near the university there is a
garrison for the army. A standing army doesn't need to do anything; just being there speaks volumes about power and control.
And yet the students were eager to debate in English on every

conceivable topic. One of my hosts told me that the universities are making every effort to sustain a democratic culture.

Democratic debate never flowered under Mao Tse-Tung and his successors. Quite the opposite—in the first five years after Mao announced the creation of the People's Republic of China, in Tiananmen Square on October 1, 1949, 800,000 people were killed. Coercive, state-sponsored collective farming has been credited with killing up to forty million people in the 1960s. During the Cultural Revolution, the Red Guard is said to have killed millions (exact figures are difficult to secure). Mao's legacy was one of brutally forced uniformity. Mao is thought to have been the principal inspiration for Pol Pot in his own forced collectivization in Cambodia, where the Khmer Rouge may have killed as many as two million people. One of the sayings of the Khmer Rouge was, "Losing you is not a loss; keeping you is not a gain."

Very limited, circumscribed "democracy" has, since the 1970s, made some show of progress in China. Deng Xiaoping, for example, explicitly advocated democracy, though it was to be a contest held in a space confined by four lines. Some likened this to baseball, only the four lines were socialism, the rule of the proletariat, a combination of Marxism-Maoism, and party leadership. But while there are not enormous signs of hope for democracy among top political leadership, there is more hope among students. The scholars and students made me think: Losing a person in China is a genuine, grievous loss. And gaining a person, as when you gain a friend in China, is a great gain indeed.

As I walked in Tiananmen Square, that place where the state launched a brutal crackdown on the student movement for democracy on June 4, 1989, I was heartened by something that will seem altogether trivial: the tourist souvenirs. The only place I saw Mao's *Red Book* and other cultural revolutionary materials during my visit was for sale as nostalgic, sometimes kitschy tourist art. I bought cigarette lighters for two economists back home which bore Mao's face (bright colors), and they play the revolutionary anthem when you light up. Perhaps such irreverent disregard of Mao's bloody legacy is a small sign that things are changing, even if this must happen one person and one university at a time.

Racism and the Woods

UP IN NORTHERN MINNESOTA THIS SUMMER IN A LOVELY
cabin overlooking a nice lake, a dozen or more philosophers from
St. Olaf and Carleton Colleges met to discuss racism and race
issues in general, beginning with the most fundamental question
of all: Does race exist? The discussion was led by a prominent
philosopher, Jorge Garcia, from Boston. Professor Garcia (who
described himself as Black Hispanic) challenged us with arguments for and against the thesis that race is a social construct; perhaps "race" refers to a real, objective kind or sort of human being;
perhaps it is a social invention and projection, as in "the line of
the equator," which "exists" in the sense that it is a projection of
cartographers but it does not possess an existence independent
of our map-making. Another way of putting his question would
be: Is ethnicity in the eye of the beholder? Professor Garcia is
known for embracing the view that racism involves an interior
vice or (not to mince words) a sin. His work presents racism as
a vile desecration of our humanity whether or not it—"race" or
"ethnicity"—is in the eye of the beholder. Note that in the following depiction of the vile nature of racism, Professor Garcia
does not commit himself about whether race actually exists as
some objective, completely independent reality:

> My proposal is that we conceive of racism as funda-
> mentally a vicious kind of racially based disregard for

the welfare of certain people. In its central and most vicious form, it is a hatred, ill-will, directed against a person or persons on account of their assigned race. In a derivative form, one is a racist when one either does not care at all or does not care enough (as morality requires) or does not care in the right ways about people assigned to a certain racial group, where this disregard is based on racial classification. Racism, then, is something that essentially involves not our beliefs and their rationality or irrationality, but our wants, intentions, likes, and dislikes and their distance from the moral virtues.

The attitude that informs racism, according to Garcia, is clearly evident in forms of malice, but racism may also be fueled by certain callous, uncaring, indifferent, disdainful, and contemptuous responses—even in the form of unresponsiveness. The sin of racism involves a set of disparaging attitudes towards those who are assigned a derogatory position, and the truth of his thesis does not depend upon whether or not race is a matter of pure social construction.

I believe Professor Garcia is fundamentally correct to focus on the evil underlying and fueling racism and not to privilege what looks like the prior, natural question of whether "race" is a construct or not. Clearly, "race" is a construct in many historical contexts, where it was designed with evil intentions. Take the recent genocide in Rwanda between the Hutus and Tutsis. They speak the same language and have the same religion. The chief difference between the two groups (insofar as they were ever completely separate; intermarriage was common) involved occupations: the Tutsis were herders and the Hutus were farmers. Rwanda was a German colony in 1885, but after World War I it became subject to Belgian rule. The Belgians introduced a "nasal index" to separate the two peoples and reduce their interaction.

The nasal index is a measurement of the length and width of the nose. The Belgians used this measurement to label those with longer, narrower noses (those they thought more closely resembled European noses) as Tutsi. Skin tone and even number of cattle owned were also used to make the distinction between Tutsi and Hutu, which was recorded on mandatory ID cards. Upon gaining their freedom in 1962, the two communities were in radical, sometimes violent tension. In the late 1980s and early 1990s, the Hutu majority unleashed a massive political campaign to support Hutu purity. The Tutsis were classified as inferior, and Hutus were armed with weapons. The groups that carried out the subsequent genocide were called the *Interahamwe* ("those who work together"), and the killing was code named *umuganda* ("public work"). In a hundred days, especially in April of 1994, a total of 800,000 people were killed.

When there is talk of ethnic purity or pride or integrity, I suggest it is always a good idea to consider what else is being discussed, and the manner in which it is discussed. When "race" and "ethnicity" are being used to affirm the rights of those who are being marginalized (or worse), or to preserve an important heritage, well and good. Matters shift otherwise. The Belgians regarded the people of the Congo as a different race; they were not Europeans. Whether or not the people of the Congo were (and are) a different "race" does not change the fact that Belgium turned the Congo into a slave state from 1885 onward, and the Belgians' brutal practices may have killed half the population (10 million people).

During our retreat with Professor Garcia, we wrestled at one point with the difficulty of defining Hispanic culture and identity. One prominent feature of being Hispanic (it was proposed) is that it involves taking pride in one's Iberian descent (being a descendent from the Portuguese or Spanish). Surely this is defensible and honorable. However, it is not without problems.

For example, the role of the Spanish and Portuguese in the slave trade and in the conquest of the Americas is deeply troubling. While the importation of Africans as slaves into the thirteen British colonies was extensive and shameful (an estimated 750,000, mostly in the American South), the total coerced migration of Africans to the Americas over 400 years was around 12 to 15 million people, with about one third going to Brazil (4–5 million) and half (6–7.5 million) into the Caribbean basin— which were all established as Iberian holdings (though some slaves also went to the British islands Barbados and Jamaica). The brutality of the Atlantic "middle passage"—from capture in Africa to arrival in the Americas—is estimated to have led to the death of about half of the people in transit. Thus 6 million imported slaves may have meant 12 million people began the voyage across the Atlantic. One could go on to consider the Catholic Monarchs of the Iberian peninsula and their treatment of Jews and Moors. The point is that the legacy of racism and oppression can creep into many different communities; the past should humble us.

What about condemning racism as a "sin"? Garcia himself uses the word in an article entitled "Racism and Racial Discourse." The word may not carry the same force in Western culture that it once did. You can glimpse the horror of being guilty of sin in a passage in Evelyn Waugh's *Brideshead Revisited,* when one of the characters laments that she is "living in sin." While the passage concerns sexual ethics, certainly a case of sustained racism would be a powerful, even more profound case of what counts as "living in sin."

> 'Living in sin'; not just doing wrong, as I did when I went to America; doing wrong, knowing it is wrong, stopping doing it, forgetting. That's not what they mean. . . . *Living in sin,* with sin, by sin, for sin, every

hour, every day, year in, year out. Waking up with sin in the morning, seeing the curtains drawn on sin, bathing it, dressing it, clipping diamonds to it, feeding it, showing it round, giving it a good time, putting it to sleep at night . . . if it's fretful. . . . Mummy dying with it; Christ dying with it, nailed hand and foot. . . .

"Sin" (which is often defined as a wrong committed against God, nature, or will) may not have the desired impact in an utterly secular context, but Garcia was driving at what I think is a defining mark of racism: *it involves violating something sacred.* In nursing or perpetuating racism, one winds up participating in what the Waugh character describes in sick, cloying, poisonous terms; it involves nursing a sustained desecration of another person.

When we finished three sessions with Professor Garcia we went to a nearby town for drinks and dinner. Jorge was the only person of African descent in the bar; everyone else would be classified as "white" or "Caucasian" or "European American." There was no visible tension or disrespect or lack of caring that night. We were a group of scholars out on the town as friends. But if someone had used a racial slur, it would not have mattered to us whether "race" is a social construction. We would have known that in an otherwise peaceful Minnesota village there was a sin being nursed, a sin that kills the soul.

Now *That* Is an Interesting Machine Gun

———

AT A RECENT DINNER PARTY, A MACHINE GUN WAS PASSED around the room, followed eventually by a switchblade and some very fine coffee. The mood was festive, and struck me as pacific and good humored, though I was a bit worried when the host set ablaze some cognac intended for desert but instead threatened to scorch the tablecloth and a guest. Fortunately there were no explosives (that I was aware of) on the table. I am not a stranger to weapons. When we were just boys, one of my brothers had a machine gun. Fortunately, it was never used to harm anyone, though it was employed in a rather dramatic way when my brother decided that my toy wooden fort should be put to the test. I was glad that I was not present during my brother's "successful assault" on the tiny wooden structure.

From time to time, it is possible to grow up with little direct exposure to violence. In the case of my family, my brothers, sisters, and I each managed to get to 18 years of age before any of us saw any real physical violence. (Matters shifted, however, after some of us passed the 18-year mark; two of my brothers were in the U.S. Army in Vietnam.) But it is sobering (to put it mildly) that in the last century wars have been responsible for about forty million deaths; and genocide, state-sponsored executions, and mass murder are accountable for 170 million. There are, of course, all sorts of different levels of horror involved, but I find one of the most depressing to be the abuse of children.

The victimization of children in war would not have surprised the ancient Greeks. The Trojan War, the most ancient and significant warfare "celebrated" in Greek poetry, was begun and ended with the sacrifice of a child. The most famous is Agamemnon's sacrifice of his daughter Iphigenia at the start of the war, in order to appease the gods and bring about wind so that Agamemnon's army might speed to Troy. At the end of the war, Trojan children, especially males, were killed along with the men. In modern times, children are both directly sacrificed in war and used as warriors. There are now about 300,000 "child soldiers"—that is, soldiers under the age of 18—in the world. In fact, over fifty countries now recruit children into their armed forces; some of them are 17 and fairly close to standard "military age," but some are as young as 7 to 10. The case against using children in the military is, I think, massive. As Archbishop Desmond Tutu observes, "It is immoral that adults should want children to fight their wars for them. . . . There is simply no excuse, no acceptable argument for arming children." Still, the United Nations and other groups have only slowly reached the stage of enforcing the ban on this use of boys and girls for war.

The legacy of violence by humans against humans makes a powerful case that violence is both normal and natural. But there is a tradition that stretches from ancient Greece to the present disputing the claim that this violence is natural even if it is normal or pervasive. Plato, Aristotle, and, years later, Augustine, articulated accounts of human nature according to which warfare was secondary; the first state of the body, and the natural state of the soul-body relationship, is one of concord and peace.

In *The City of God* Augustine offers this somewhat amusing portrait of the peace and integrity of the body.

> If anyone were to hang upside-down, the position of
> the body and arrangement of the limbs is undoubtedly
> perverted, because what should be on top, according to
> the dictates of nature, is underneath, and what nature
> intends to be underneath is on top. This perverted at-
> titude disturbs the peace of the flesh, and causes distress
> for that reason. For all that, the breath is at peace with
> its body and is busily engaged for its preservation; that
> is why there is something to endure the pain. And even
> if the breath is finally driven from the body by its dis-
> tresses, still, as long as the framework of the limbs holds
> together, what remains retains a kind of peace among the
> bodily parts; hence there is still something to hang there.

I do not want to endorse the view that for a human being to
hang upside-down is a perversion, but I commend the thesis that
healthy bodily integrity is prior and thus more basic than violence
and war. As Augustine pointed out, warfare is a complex act requiring immense health and interior resolve, harmony, and power.
Without some kind of antecedent or prior peace, there could be
no war. All three philosophers argued that evil results from striving to achieve good (security, power, and health, for example) in
the wrong way or for the wrong reason. Augustine in particular
saw acts of cruelty as perpetrated out of a misperception of justice.
For example, a murderer may be trying to effect revenge, which in
essence is a perverse or twisted form of "justice." Plato, Aristotle,
and Augustine were not pacifists. If they were alive today, they
might even recommend that, in some circumstances, it is a good
thing to have an efficient machine gun. But the weight of their
philosophy was towards privileging nonviolence and securing a
good justice that would fulfill our human nature.

Whatever you think of the ancient attempts at understanding
human nature as oriented to the good, the International Court of

Justice (the U.N.'s highest judicial body) recognizes that human beings can commit crimes against humanity. Arguably, this involves the claim that human beings can be so cruel that they do acts which violate humanity itself. On this view, human nature is a good, not to be violated, and we human beings need to take action against persons who commit genocide, rape, and so on, whether or not those persons were working within the sanctions of their own nation. Obviously, today, the International Court of Justice (I.C.J.) is limited in power (this was not helped by the U.S. withdrawing from the World Judicial Body on March 10, 2005), and there are glaring cases of criminals against humanity going unpunished. Idi Amin, former dictator of Uganda, killed more than 300,000 people, yet he lived unpunished until he died naturally in a Saudi villa. But there is some progress in seeking to secure the work of the I.C.J. and to expose inhumane acts publicly. When Hitler sought to place his own genocidal campaign in world perspective, he is known to have asked (rhetorically), "Who remembers the Armenians?" He used the fact that the world largely ignored the one million Armenians, killed by the Ottoman Empire in 1915, to argue that the world would largely ignore his own final solution. Fortunately, we do remember the Armenians today, and countless others who have perished unjustly.

The dinner party with a machine gun was hosted by a retired naval intelligence officer and his wife. They were not angry warlords, and I saw no relish in their contemplating the harm that could be unleashed by the machine gun and the switchblade. But the incident with the machine gun did make me think of the line in Isaiah in which the people of Israel look to God to inspire them to beat weapons into farm equipment—ploughshares and pruning hooks. Driving home, I wished a Heavenly Father would do to all weapons—on this planet as well as those we humans have placed in space—what my earthly father did with my brother's machine gun: he dismantled it.

A Modest Defense of Magic

"MAGIC" HAS HAD A MIXED ROLE IN WESTERN HISTORY. If by "magic" you are referring to Witchcraft and Satanism, then it is clear that more people were executed in Europe on charges of magic than in the course of the entire Inquisition. The Inquisition killed around 5,000 people, whereas between 80,000 and 100,000 were executed in what has been called the Witch Craze, which lasted from the late fifteenth to the late seventeenth century in Europe. In popular culture today, one can still see a deep suspicion of magic in the opposition by some conservative Christians to the Harry Potter literature and films. Some of these conservatives are inspired by the New Testament portrait of the early church burning books of magic. "Many of those who practiced magic brought their books together and burned them in the sight of all" (Acts 19:19, NKJV). But the opposition to magic, even among Christians, has not been consistent, and some Christian philosophers even practiced a modest form of what was called good magic.

The distinction between good magic and bad magic was made by Marsilio Ficino (1433–1499) in the Italian renaissance. Ficino argued that the prohibitions in the Bible against magic were all cases of when people used charms or spells in the cause of Satan and malice. Magic was also bad when it was used simply for non-malicious self-advancement. And, too, it was important to distinguish between proper religion, which (according to Ficino) consists of worship, virtue, and petitionary prayer, and religion which is really just a quasi-magical attempt to control God. But Ficino did think that the soul's pilgrimage to God involved a kind of falling in love which he thought of in terms of magic. For him, God is to be understood principally in terms of beauty and goodness. To come to the love of God involves being enchanted or coming under the spell of beauty and goodness, first in creation and then, step by step, by being drawn to the Creator and Author of beauty and goodness. By his lights, this was not first and foremost accomplished by rigorous proofs or mechanical arguments. Falling under the spell of God involves *good magic*.

I believe there is some truth to Ficino's teaching. Very late in a course I was teaching in ethics, a senior came into my office and asked why he should care at all about any of the topics we were discussing. Why should he care about the suffering or happiness of anyone else? I replied: Imagine that someone comes to you in extraordinary pain. It is clear that the person has been savagely beaten and will perish unless she gets immediate help. Imagine further *that you feel absolutely nothing*. Wouldn't you have to say that, in this situation, you or some part of you is dead? After a long silence he said "Yes." And then we went on to discuss his next paper, what he wanted to do after graduation, and so on.

Looking back on this exchange, I would have to say that I did not present him with a rigorous argument. He would have been perfectly within his rights to reply that he was *not* dead, he simply had no concern for the suffering of others. I was appealing, instead, to his feelings. Or, in the spirit of Ficino, I was pleading with him to feel the importance of goodness and beauty, and the horror of being completely blank emotionally. G. K. Chesterton once said that some people are not able to think their way out of certain self-contained enclosures. Recall the old story of the man who thought he was dead. He goes to his doctor. The doctor convinces him that a corpse does not bleed. The doctor then gives the man a pin prick, causing some bleeding. Rather than conclude he is not dead, the man shouts, "Dead men *do* bleed!" This would be a case where a spell must be broken; the man needs air and a new enchantment and allegiance to life. Quarreling over the definition of "death" would probably not do the trick.

One of the more wonderful literary uses of magic in teaching ethics is in T. H. White's stories of Merlyn. In *The Sword in the Stone,* Merlyn teaches Arthur the ways of the world, good and evil, by turning him into a fish. Later he is transformed into a squirrel. He looks at the world from the standpoint of different species. And in White's *The Book of Merlyn,* which he wrote in the early part of World War II, Arthur is instructed on the evils of totalitarianism, the good of dignity and respect, and the appeal of a just peace by being magically put in conversation with other animals. This is an extraordinary use of good magic. White was keenly aware of the horrors of war and he used his imagination to engage readers in trying to think through all the values in play. In his diary of November 14, 1940, he wrote of his plan to portray old King Arthur entering into a discussion of war with animals. "They must decide to talk thoroughly over, during Arthur's long retirement underground, the relation of man to the other animals, in the hope of getting a new angle on his problem from this. Such, indeed, was Merlyn's original objective in introducing him to the animals in the first place." You may think this is preposterous nonsense. But White was, I think, using his imagination as a weapon, a means of cajoling us out of lethargy and causing us to take seriously our relations to each other and the world as a whole.

Earlier, on October 23, 1940, White wrote about the ugliness of Nazism. "The timbre of the voices which sing about Hitler and death is a sneering, nasal mock-timbre. Devils in hell must sing like this." Over against that horror, White follows the good magic tradition of Ficino and others by asking us to renew a master-pupil relationship with a somewhat befuddled, but gentle, wise, peace-loving wizard.

T. H. White may have written children's stories, but one might also keep in mind the way in which it is sometimes in childhood that the first struggle between good and evil—or, if you will, good and bad magic—takes place. The Nazis preyed on children, channeling boys into the Hitler Youth and girls into the League of German Maidens, drawing them all together in dehumanizing rallies where, among other things, they burned books.

Enemies Are at the Gate,
but Friends Are at the Door!

—◦—

I HAD A BAD DREAM THIS SUMMER. YOU MIGHT TOO IF you spent your last waking moments reading about a monstrous beast, hungry and lurking in a dead valley. At dawn, when the nightmare was coming to a close, I was greeted with a strange mix of alarm and comfort. I heard, or dreamed I heard, a proclamation: "There are enemies at the gate, but friends are at the door!" I suspect that the dream and proclamation were produced, in part, by J. R. R. Tolkien's *The Lord of the Rings*, published in 1954–55. This summer marks my third encounter with the fantasy world of Tolkien (1892–1973) with its orcs, goblins, wizards, elves, and the mythic, enchanting hobbits.

I read the Rings Trilogy for the first time in the early 1970s in England. I had just given up taking hallucinogenic drugs and discovered, to my surprise, that Tolkien's world was far more interesting than anything I had ever dreamed of, much less hallucinated. I made a pilgrimage to where Tolkien lived (Oxford), began smoking a pipe, and used a walking stick. But when I read the Trilogy a second time, in my mid-twenties, things became a bit embarrassing. Back in the States, I used wood and cloth to construct a huge dragon on the roof of a house, and then, in a knight's outfit with wooden sword and shield, I attacked it, crying "Elendil! I am with you, Gandalf!" No controlled substances (other than Tolkien) were involved.

Now, as a late forty-something college teacher, I don't think it would be a very good idea (with or without tenure) to re-enact Tolkien's War of the Ring or, more specifically, Gandalf's battle with the Balrog on the Bridge of Khazad-dûm. Tolkien's portrait of enmity and enemies in the Trilogy is enough to give anyone bad dreams. I have no desire to wind up in Shelob's Lair or to have a run-in with the Nine Black Riders, or to have to rely upon Gollum as a guide. Since we live in a world where there is no shortage of malevolence, I half wonder whether there isn't some reason for writers and filmmakers to pause and cut back on populating our imagination with yet more fresh pictures of evil, no matter how ingenious. Once you have spent quality time with Caligula and Iago, why brood over Sauron and his red eye? We have no trouble whatsoever worrying about enemies at our gate even when they aren't there. Probably our worst enemies are those who have crept through the gate ages ago and taken up residence inside us, much in the way that an older moral tradition spoke of the Seven Deadly Sins. Do we really need new, inventive images of evil to plague our dreams?

Maybe we need Tolkien's world of evil because of this predicament: that it seems easier for many of us to imagine evil rather than goodness. Tolkien, by contrast, seems equally at home with both. He deals brilliantly with evil shadows and cold death, but he also gives us a host of characters such as Gandalf, the hobbits Frodo and Sam, Galadriel, and Treebeard. Tolkien gives us lots of evil and, at the same time, a greater good. He gives us an image of the Good that shines all the brighter when it is threatened and even almost overwhelmed by a gnawing, relentless evil.

Tolkien needed no reminder of unhappiness and terror. He did much of the writing of the Trilogy for his son, Christopher, during his service in the British army in World War II. Tolkien himself served in the British army in France in the First World War. C. S. Lewis speculated that Tolkien's depiction of Mordor stemmed from his exposure to trench warfare. The background of the Trilogy is the horror of war, with its weapons, its privation of food, sight, and hearing, and its disorienting smell—while in the foreground one sees friendship and courage alongside humor and mirth.

I suspect one of the reasons for the Trilogy's huge success in the mid-60s was because of the Vietnam War and my generation's hunger for a picture of goodness amid all the bloodshed and confusion that entered into our homes over the evening news. Tolkien may have achieved his massive readership, too, because of a backlash against a kind of malaise (however hip and intelligent) that came from European existentialist writers. I doubt I was alone in rejecting Jean-Paul Sartre's portrait of human life in the appropriately titled novel *Nausea*, in which a main character reports, "I don't have adventures. This is not a mere question of the definition of terms." I prefer instead to think of the opening scene of *The Hobbit* (a prelude to the Ring Trilogy, published in 1937), when the wizard Gandalf sees Bilbo sitting outside his house. Gandalf reports, "I am looking for someone to share in an adventure...." Those who travel through Tolkien's world are not spared from evil, but neither are they spared from hope.

Apart from being a professor of Anglo-Saxon and of English language and literature at Oxford University, Tolkien was a great student of fairy stories. By his lights, many fairy stories are built around the theme of escape. The ultimate escape, for Tolkien, was escape from death. Now, Tolkien was not a life-denying Don, desperate to leave the earth in an apocalyptic rapture. The love of this life runs through the Trilogy and Tolkien's other tales, histories, translations, and essays. The inventor of the character Old Tom Bombadil had to have been a merry fellow, even if he also invented Saruman and Sauron. Still, Tolkien was a Christian who, along with his friends C. S. Lewis and Dorothy Sayers, thought that the end of all our stories would be what he called *eucatastrophic,* a kind of unexpected, joyful deliverance or escape from evil and the finality of death. He coined the word "eucatastrophic" to identify an event that is the exact opposite of a tragedy. In his essay "On Fairy-Stories," Tolkien writes, "The eucatastrophic tale is the true form of fairy-tale, and its highest function.... It does not deny the existence of sorrow and failure: the possibility of these is necessary to the joy of deliverance; it denies (in the face of much evidence, if you will) universal final defeat ... giving a fleeting glimpse of Joy, Joy beyond the walls of the world, poignant as grief." I think it is this joyful conception of the way in which the happiness of this life can serve as a token of a greater joy that gives Tolkien's work such transporting beauty, humor, and nerve.

In the course of making my way through the Trilogy again I feel no temptation to dress up as a wizard or knight. I am instead stirred by an image of a world in which the Good is not boring or less interesting than evil. The Good shines. It suggests an escape from evil, whether or not the escape will, in the end, be successful. In the midst of Tolkien's world of dark powers, he gives us an image of friends at the door.

"The hobbits bowed low," Tolkien wrote. Frodo is taking leave of a warrior who has offered him aid and comfort in a time of great peril. "'Most gracious host,' said Frodo, 'it was said to me ... that I should find friendship upon the way, secret and unlooked for. Certainly I looked for no such friendship as you have shown. To have found it turns evil to great good.'"

Shakespeare, Actually

LAUGHTER HAS BEEN STUDIED ON MANY FRONTS. FROM A physiological point of view, it involves the contraction of about fifteen facial muscles, breathing is often altered, and sometimes the zygomatic major causes the lips to form a "smile." Theories of humor and wit abound. My least favorite is that laughter involves a "disguised snarl" (Konrad Lorenz); an equally depressing account of humor comes from Max Beerbohm, who identified "two elements in the public's humor: delight in suffering, [and] contempt for the unfamiliar." Shakespeare's comedies present a different picture: laughter sometimes flows from pure benevolence.

Medieval thought on the nature of love sometimes distinguished between *benevolent love*—which involves a desire and pleasure in the flourishing of the beloved—and *unitive love.* Unitive love involves the desire for and pleasure in union with the beloved, whether this involves eros or the non-erotic companionship of friends or family. Many a tragedy is built on the conflict or imbalance between these two loves, as when a person's unitive love is stronger than benevolent love. But when the two loves come together, as they often do in Shakespearean comedy, there is often gaiety and levity, a non-possessive, romantic delight and laughter. In *Twelfth Night*, for example, the lovers delight in their discovery of one another, whereas the central character in the play who fails to find love does so because he is too possessive of himself and of the one he pursues romantically. Malvolio is tricked into thinking that the one he loves (Olivia) desires him. Malvolio entertains the following picture of life with Olivia:

> Having been three months married to her, sitting in my state . . . Calling my officers about me in my branch'd velvet gown; having come from a day-bed where I have left Olivia sleeping . . . And then to have the humor of state; and after a demure travel of regard—telling them I know my place as I would they should do theirs. . . .
>
> (Act II, Scene V)

Malvolio imagines his great success as a lover, but the pleasure is in his own powers. "Olivia" is not, for Malvolio, a living person but a shadow. There is no real laughter or mirth here.

Shakespearean themes of love and laughter are alive and well in some contemporary films. The movie *Love Actually* (2003) may seem an unlikely place to look for Shakespeare or even elevated, rather Christian views about love. After all, the film seems to take a relaxed view on pornography, profanity, and group sex. The "spiritual" or Christian elements may seem quite superficial: there are respectful (non-sarcastic, non-ironic) portraits of a church wedding, a funeral, and a nativity play. The hymn "Silent Night" is played during a pivotal scene of confession and friendship, and an overjoyed British bachelor exclaims, "Praise the Lord!" as he meets several available Wisconsin women. One of the characters is even portrayed as having an uncanny, almost magical, way of facilitating love: Rowan Atkinson plays the role of a kind of angel. But all these matters to one side, you can still find a core Shakespearean message of laughter's residence in love.

There are many stories in the film that are interconnected. The most "normal" successful courtship is, in a way, the most unconventional. John and Judy meet at work, get to know each other gradually, and then marry. Their work, however, is as stand-ins for a pornographic movie. The humor lies, in part, in how their ordinary but amusing, genuine love makes the pornographic framework ridiculous and un-sexy. The first kiss they share fully clothed when John walks Judy home *is* sexy, whereas the other nude shots are comparatively funny, principally because of their irony.

The two relationships that do not work seem to fail because of a refusal of humor, a failure to bring together unitive and benevolent loves. Sarah is smitten with Karl, who loves her in return. But she cannot (or at least she does not) share with Karl the plight of her handicapped brother. The brother-sister relationship is treated with wonderful sensitivity (they embrace in the last scene we see of them in the film), but Sarah's failure to confide in Karl and to give him a chance to interact with the brother means there will be no real union.

The other failure involves infidelity. Harry and Karen have a comfortable marriage and two children. But Harry is clearly flattered and then easily swept away by a flirtation at the office with Mia. The Harry and Karen characters reconcile in the end, but it is clear that they have a way to go in order to find—or rediscover—a fresh love for each other. All the other lovers (the Prime Minister and his personal assistant; a non-Portuguese-speaking British writer and his non-English-speaking Portuguese maid; and so on) involve absurdities (singing Christmas carols with a policeman; courting a lover in a car with a child dressed up as a sea creature; and so on). Laughter is at every turn. The film culminates in scenes at London's Heathrow Airport where the movie's lovers and friends jest and play. This is pure Shakespeare. In *The Tempest*, when Miranda and Ferdinand fall in love, they play.

In Shakespearean romantic comedies not everyone's story ends happily. In *Twelfth Night*, Malvolio is not the only one left out in the cold. But some of the best exits by characters who have not found romantic love happen without bitterness. The clown's song at the end of *Twelfth Night* is a kind of celebration of creation and theater. He has no lover and yet there is mirth in his song. Here are the last four lines:

> A great while ago the world begun,
> With hey ho, the wind and the rain,
> But that's all one, our play is done,
> And we'll strive to please you every day.

(Act V, Scene I)

It would be hard to sing that song while snarling, delighting in the suffering of others, or feeling contempt for the unfamiliar.

The Passion and
the Happiness of the Christ

——•——

THE OPENING LINES IN LEO TOLSTOY'S NOVEL *ANNA
Karenina* are, "All happy families resemble one another. But
each unhappy family is unhappy in its own way." I don't know
whether Tolstoy's claim is true, but what he might be getting at
is that in families where there is real, tangible happiness, it appears that people are able to act as they really are; in short, they
are able to be themselves. Families that are happy may resemble
each other in providing the air and space in which individuals
can stretch themselves without fear. By way of contrast, in many
unhappy families there always seems to be something distinc-
tive preventing this liberty—the self-absorbed, overbearing father; the angry, unpredictable sister; the uncle who dominates
every possible conversation; and so on. Something similar may
be true about religion.

I believe there are happy and unhappy Christian religious
traditions and communities in every denomination. On the one
hand, there are Christian contexts in which persons seem to
flourish, to stretch without fear, to be themselves, and to find
honest fulfillment. Thomas Aquinas wrote that the goal of grace
is to perfect and fulfill nature, rather than to destroy it. And
before Aquinas, Jesus himself claimed that his desire was for
us to have life and to have it in abundance. On the other hand,
there have been unhappy perversions and failures in so-called

Christian communities where God is pictured as a self-absorbed, angry, and unpredictable, dominating reality. Some of the anti-Semitism generated by people calling themselves Christian is particularly odious from a Christian point of view in which (again, according to the Jesus of the Gospels) our key commandment is to love others. And this is a commandment, not an invitation.

The advent of the Mel Gibson movie *The Passion of the Christ* has stirred concern among many about this particularly ugly side of "Christianity." After all, in the High Middle Ages, Jewish communities were sometimes subjected to great violence in the season of Easter, when the passion of Christ was re-enacted. We should not forget that the first, disastrous People's Crusade to "liberate" Jerusalem was prefaced in the eleventh century by the massacre of Jewish communities in the Rhine Valley.

I don't think *The Passion of the Christ* is all bad or concerned only with an unhappy Christianity. The faces he captures on film are extraordinary. Satan is perfectly horrible; he makes Gollum in *The Lord of the Rings* look good. Judas, Peter, Pilate, John, and both Mary the Mother and Mary Magdalene are transfixing. The relationship between Jesus and his mother is attractive.

Even so, I have two difficulties with the film, one cinematic and the other theological. From the standpoint of the film itself, the relentless whipping and beating, the skin laceration, the endless mocking, and the extraordinary, almost supernatural, flow of blood makes *The Passion of the Christ* into a horror movie. I don't deny that Good Friday was horrifying. But such horror is different from what you find in "horror movies," where there is a tendency to treat monstrous events as vaguely comic, with a blend of irony and melodrama. At Jesus' death, when his side is pierced, blood starts gushing out with the quantity and force of a fireman's water hose; the result is what some film critics might call a "splatter movie."

Apart from such eerie, over-the-top cinematic devices, there is the general problem that typical horror movies invite one to take pleasure in destructive powers. The monster is supposed to look like unrealistic, organized stupidity, a beast that is the object of a blend of humor and pity. The opportunity to relish the depiction of Jesus' suffering can be provided both by this dramatic, spellbinding side of the spectacle itself, but it can also develop from a religious motive. The suffering of Jesus may be seen as a sign of love: Jesus loves the world so much that he undergoes a soul-destroying degree of degradation and defilement in order to draw people to the kingdom of God. But, in a misunderstanding of Jesus' suffering, love of his selfless gift can lead one to value or take pleasure in the crucifixion. On this point, my worries turn theological.

There is no way to plausibly deny the centrality of the crucifixion of Christ in Christianity. But it is important to understand the crucifixion in perspective. For most Christian theology, historically, it is not just the passion and crucifixion that is redemptive, but the whole of Christ's life. This includes Christ's birth, teaching and healing, miracles, friendships, regard for the stranger, and yes, his death and resurrection. Christ is believed to have been so full of life and God's love that he overcame evil and provided a way for the world to give up its vanity and cruelty. The incarnation, on this view, is more about loving and restoring life than hatred of evil; it is about establishing what, in Tolstoy's terms, would be a happy rather than unhappy family— in my terms, a happy religion.

My worry is that the film takes us to a spiritual ground zero where one is given very little guidance for understanding the positive teaching of Christ. In the ancient world, crucifixion was commonplace. It was even regarded as entertaining. If you went to the Coliseum in Rome, criminals were often crucified during the lunch hour, which marked an intermission between the morning show of people being killed by "exposure"(wild beasts) and the afternoon gladiatorial games. Christ's torture and barbaric death may have been more brutal than others, but what early Christians celebrated was the overcoming of this form of murder and, even more importantly, death itself.

While the ancients may not have found the violence of the cross unusual, what they did find unusual and deeply attractive was the nonviolence of Christ's life and teaching. Christian joy was, I think, not in the cross, but before and after the cross or, if you will, through it. The New Testament describes Christ as enduring the shame of the cross for "the joy set before him" (Hebrews 12:2, NIV). At Good Friday, some Christians venerate the cross by kissing it; and, indeed, in the film Jesus is seen embracing the cross almost as though it was a friend. But what is pivotal to most Christian theology is that the cross as an instrument of torture, and death itself, are defeated by and through the love of God; apart from the occasional Christian cult, for the central Christian tradition there is no pleasure in Jesus' torment. Kissing the cross may be a symbolic or sacramental way of kissing Christ, or even of enacting a ritual reversal of the kiss of Judas who betrayed Christ. It is not kissing torment. If it were a veneration of suffering, it would be a case of theological sadism and a dangerous religious accommodation of violence. And in a world where people have been persecuted in the name of Christ, such an accommodation must be avoided at all costs.

The film does portray Jesus in happier times. There is a wonderful scene of him building a table and playfully jesting with his mother. Jesus is shown sharing wine and bread with the disciples. There is even a resurrection at the end of the film in which the Risen Christ seems serene, strong, composed, and resolute. But these scenes are on the border, the outskirts of what is the central theme of the film: a sequence of injustice, torture, dying, and death. Consider a contemporary film in which there is also something like a death and resurrection, *The Lord of the Rings*. Gandalf the wizard undergoes dramatic combat with a beast and seems either to die or undergo an extraordinary purgation before he is dramatically restored, or reborn, with immense power for good. It may seem unfair to compare an epic fantasy with a film on religious history, but Tolkien's books and their film version do take evil seriously. Tolkien's own experience in the First World War, with all its horrors, is the likely inspiration for much of the evil in his work.

Near the end, when evil is defeated, Gandalf laughs with Frodo and Sam. This is beautifully portrayed in the film. In the book, here is the crucial passage: "'A great Shadow has departed,' said Gandalf, and then he laughed, and the sound was like music, or like water in a parched land; and as he listened the thought came to Sam that he had not heard laughter, the pure sound of merriment, for days upon days without count. It fell upon his ears like the echo of all the joys he had ever known."

I cannot imagine Mel Gibson's Jesus laughing after the resurrection, and I suspect this is because both Jesus and we are literally exhausted by the horrors of the passion. The film couldn't depict Christ laughing after the resurrection because, while it does convey something of Jesus' loving teaching and triumph, its vast weight is more on the mock trial and cruel breaking of an innocent person.

But the New Testament's full picture of Jesus suggests a different side. Yes, Jesus underwent the agony and humiliation of the cross. But after the resurrection, Jesus joins some people at a dinner party (Luke 24); there is even what might be described as a beach picnic with the resurrected Jesus (John 21). I can't help but think of this Jesus laughing. Recall that this is the same Jesus whose first miracle is turning water into wine.

Is it possible to turn water into wine with a straight face? Or would children ever seek to be with an adult who lacked mirth?

I suspect Gandalf's laughing, wise presence was probably modeled by Tolkien (who was a Christian) on Christ. The emphasis of the New Testament is on the contagious, liberating force of Christ's love and happiness, in which joy is seen as bigger than sorrow. By putting the vast resources of modern filmmaking on the immensity of the sorrow and cruelty of the passion, Mel Gibson and filmgoers have a more perplexing time finding a place for the love, happiness, and joy that made the passion profoundly human and divine.

Is the Detective Chief Inspector
in Love Today?

THE MOST WIDELY KNOWN DETECTIVE IN EARLY MODERN literature is Sherlock Holmes, the creation of a doctor, Sir Arthur Conan Doyle, who lived in Victorian London. This literature marked a transition in English culture, as the prison conditions improved (somewhat), the death penalty was imposed less often, and there was a greater effort by public administrators to understand the psychology behind crime. In narrating the cases of an eccentric sleuth with his moodiness, love of music, and devotion to the scientific method, along with his faithful physician assistant, Doyle invited readers to consider with sympathy (and horror) the minds of murderers, and to do so across the divide of class boundaries. Doyle put on display criminal intentions and dark deeds of the privileged and showed how the "best" in society might be exposed and brought to justice through intelligence and even wit. It was largely based on a study of Holmes, along with three other detectives, that W. H. Auden formulated his famous formula for detective stories.

In a popular essay, "The Guilty Vicarage," Auden suggests that most of us who love detective fiction struggle with a sense of sin. By following the exploits of the detective we investigate how he or she exposes the guilt of those who appear innocent, and uncover the innocence of those who appear guilty. The crucial moment, for us, is that the detective exposes *someone other than ourselves* as properly guilty. Our innocence is reinforced by the following process:

> The magic formula is an innocence which is discovered to contain guilt; then a suspicion of being the guilty one; and finally a real innocence from which the guilty other has been expelled, a cure effected, not by me or my neighbors, but by the miraculous intervention of a genius from outside who removes guilt by giving knowledge of guilt.

Auden may or may not be right in this outline. Some readers of mysteries I know don't seem to be particularly prey to a deep suspicion of their own sin. But I have noticed another avenue of redemption that Auden alludes to (but does not develop) in some contemporary mysteries, especially in the novels and films involving Detective Chief Inspector Morse of the Thames Valley Police in Oxford, England. (For those readers who are skeptical about the wisdom of detectives, please note that Confucius was a chief of police in Lu, sixth century BCE. And, for a more recent case involving a brilliant, wise essayist, George Orwell was part of the police force in Burma.)

Morse, a creation of Colin Dexter, shares with Holmes a love of music and an irascible personality. Rather than cocaine, Morse prefers beer and scotch. Morse is not exactly a fan of feminism or women's liberation, but he has none of the misogyny of Holmes.

But in some respects, Morse does have a link with Holmes. Oxford as a city goes back at least to the tenth century, part of the medieval wall around the city is preserved, and there was a college there at least by the twelfth century. There is still a fair amount of nineteenth-century architecture about, and the tutorial system (one to one; professor-student) came into its own while Holmes was capturing criminals in London. There is also another crossover to the Victorian era, as one of the final cases that Morse takes on, "The Wench Is Dead," involved a crime committed in Holmes's time.

Morse was played to perfection in a television series by John Thaw until his untimely death, and Colin Dexter came to incorporate many of Thaw's characteristics into his novels. An abiding feature of Morse is his sadness. Amid his love for opera, his car, and his affection (often inconsistently expressed) for his assistant, Sergeant Lewis (played by Kevin Whatley), there remains a sense of unfulfillment, a feeling of loss and (especially) of unrequited love. In fact, Morse is constantly falling in love. And he is just as constantly having to face up to the relationship not working out beyond a few tantalizing but brief encounters. On some level, Morse finds the world beautiful as well as profoundly disappointing.

Why would this sadness be at all satisfying? Perhaps there are two reasons. One is that his sadness at, say, having lost the love of his life (Susan) to someone else (in *Dead On Time*), becomes a kind of witness to the original love he has for Susan. After all these years, he still loves her even though she married a rival, Henry Fallon, an Oxford Don. Second, a case can be made that many of the suspects that Morse investigates commit crime, and chiefly murder, in order to avoid some great suffering of their own: a person cannot endure being childless *(Greeks Bearing Gifts)*, or not seeking revenge *(Second Time Around)*, or not getting a famous lectureship *(Last Bus to Woodstock)*, and so on. Morse's sorrow is somehow honest. In a sense it is emblematic of justice, or of living without breaking the rules. He unmasks the criminal's false happiness or pretense to contentment, and points the way to a sadness that is reassuring and consoling on the grounds that it is grounded in a genuine reality.

I suggest, then, an extension of Auden's proposal, at least for the Detective Chief Inspector of the Thames Valley Police. The magic formula is finding that an apparent happiness, or the illusion of contentment, is based on a concealed wrong. And perhaps it also involves *our* own worry about whether our apparent happiness or contentment (or whatever our emotion happens to be) is based on a concealed wrong. But, finally, with Morse's help, we expel our pretenses and orient ourselves more to the-way-things-are, whether that involves romantic love or, as with Morse, the perpetual loss of it.

Going Up?
The Lighter Side of Christian Mysticism

THE WORD *MYSTICISM* OFTEN CONJURES UP A PICTURE OF a vague, enigmatic mist. As one of my professors used to say, "mysticism" begins with a "mist" and ends with an "ism." The title of a book published in 1914 by Evelyn Underhill, *Practical Mysticism,* may seem as contradictory as *a pacifist army.* And yet there have been pacifist armies—the Italian army that was deployed in the Balkans in the 1990s was known as such in the Italian press because of its opposition to killing and coercion. And many people who are classified in Christian tradition as "mystics" have been quite down to earth, if not worldly, and have a good sense of humor.

This earthy humor among the Christian mystics came home in a story I recently read about St. Teresa of Avila (1515–1582). Though celebrated as the author of some of the most authoritative texts on the mystical life, she certainly knew how to enjoy herself. Here is one report that captures her worldliness: "A friend was once surprised to find St. Teresa gorging herself on a partridge. 'What would people think?' asked the friend. 'Let them think whatever they want,' said Teresa. 'There's time for penance, and there's time for partridge.'"

Christian mysticism may seem opaque from the outside, but up close it can be seen as sensual and full of wit. As Goethe once remarked, Christianity is like a church with stained glass;

seen from the outside it might look dark, but seen from the inside it is full of color. Even from the inside some events—like St. Francis receiving the stigmata of Christ, bearing wounds on his hands, feet, and right side—will seem jarring. But there is also evidence of a vast fellowship among mystics or saints that is full of good humor.

Returning to St. Francis, one cannot help but relish *The Little Flowers of Saint Francis,* which contain stories of his life. Consider, for example, the tales entitled "How St. Francis Tamed the Very Fierce Wolf of Gubbio"—an account of St. Francis working out an understanding between a wolf and some villagers.

> And St. Francis said: "Brother Wolf, I want you to give me a pledge so that I can confidently believe what you promise."
>
> And as St. Francis held out his hand to receive the pledge, the wolf also raised its front paw and meekly and gently put it in St. Francis' hand as a sign that it was giving its pledge.
>
> Then St. Francis said: "Brother Wolf, I order you, in the name of the Lord Jesus Christ, to come with me now, without fear, into the town to make this peace pact in the name of the Lord."
>
> And the wolf immediately began to walk along beside St. Francis, just like a very gentle lamb. When the people saw this, they were greatly amazed, and the news spread quickly throughout the whole town, so that all of them, men as well as women, great and small, assembled on the market place, because St. Francis was there with the wolf.

There is the wonderful miracle story, "How St. Francis Made the Wine Increase in a Poor Priest's Vineyard." And the stories of St. Francis preaching to the fish and birds are all painted in bright colors: "Now at these words of St. Francis, all those birds began to open their beaks, stretch out their necks, spread their wings, and reverently bow their heads to the ground, showing by their movements and their songs that the words which St. Francis was saying gave them great pleasure." These are stories of great levity, sometimes literally; see, for example, "How St. Francis Lifted Brother Masseo in the Air."

I suggest that what we sometimes overlook about the leading contributors to the Christian mystical tradition is the amount of play involved. We tend to think of "play" in terms of either sports or children's games of make-believe. And we often think that if someone is playing, they are not serious. But there is another tradition, espoused in the nineteenth century by Johann Christoph Friedrich von Schiller, in which "play" can refer to worthwhile, serious activity that one enjoys for its own sake. In his classic work on values, *On the Aesthetic Education of Man,* Schiller writes that human beings are most mature when they play, especially when this involves beauty. Life-affirming play is preeminently found in the exchange between friends, for in an authentic friendship the individuals involved are not seeking to use the friendship for self-advancement, business, or some other end. Friendship is valued and enjoyed for its own sake. And for those whose friendship involves a religious dimension, the love shared may be said to participate in God's love for the world. As St. Aelred of Rievaulx argues in *On Spiritual Friendship* (twelfth century), God wills that there be friendship, and so the cultivation of friendship itself can be seen as a sacred undertaking.

The most powerful testimony I know to the indispensable good of friendship, and thus of play, comes from St. Teresa's classic mystical text *The Way of Perfection.* In the passage that follows, St. Teresa prays for friendship and offers some advice to her readers.

O Lord, wilt Thou not grant me the favour of giving me many who have such love for me? Truly, Lord, I would rather have these than be loved by all the kings and lords of the world—and rightly so, for such friends use every means in their power to make us lords of the whole world and to have all that is in it subject to us. When you make the acquaintance of any such persons, sisters, the Mother Prioress should employ every effort to keep you in touch with them. Love such persons as much as you like. There can be very few of them, but none the less it is the Lord's will that their goodness should be known. When one of you is striving after perfection, she will at once be told that she has no need to know such people—that it is enough for her to have God. But to get to know God's friends is a very good way of "having" Him; as I have discovered by experience, it is most helpful. For under the Lord, I owe it to such persons that I am not in hell.

It is hard to find a stronger insistence on the importance of friendship and (if Schiller is right) the vital, even life-saving importance of play among friends.

A Very Large, Magical Victorian

G. K. CHESTERTON (1874–1936) OFFERS THIS OVERVIEW OF
Victorian vices and virtues:

> The Victorian Age . . . is almost a complete contrast
> to all that is now connoted by that word. It had all the
> vices that are now called virtues: religious doubt, intel-
> lectual unrest, a hungry credulity about new things, a
> complete lack of equilibrium. It also had all the virtues
> that are now called vices: a rich sense of romance, a
> passionate desire to make the love of man and woman
> once more what it was in Eden, a strong sense of the
> absolute necessity of some significance in human life.

Chesterton outlived the Victorian era, but he held many of its
virtues and few of its vices.

Apart from the scurrilous, sometimes appalling practices
that are associated with the Victorian age (the expansion of
British imperial power, the Opium Wars, and so on), there were
in that era also figures of great compassion and insight. The
Victorian age had its scoundrels, but there were also heroines
like Florence Nightingale (known as the Lady of the Lamp),
who saved hundreds, if not thousands, through her nursing.
And there were literary geniuses like Charles Dickens (one of
the few, along with Trollope and George Eliot, who supported

themselves through their writing), who was a clear and powerful advocate for the poor. Chesterton carried on the work of Dickens and Nightingale; he was a kind of *Gentleman of the Lamp* insofar as he sought to address the moral and religious illness of the age. Thus, Chesterton was against the Boer War which (in hindsight) is very difficult to justify—Britain simply wanted to control the riches that were being claimed by Dutch settlers in South Africa. He was a "distributionist," part of a movement that sought the redistribution of wealth in England. Chesterton pitted himself against the dehumanizing mechanization of life that seemed to crush human individuality.

Chesterton was a literary critic, essayist, journalist, novelist, and poet. He had some weaknesses, to be sure. The vast amount of work he produced guarantees that not all of it is of the same quality. Between 1900 and 1936 he published one hundred books, and from 1905 till the week he died he wrote 1,535 essays for the *Illustrated London News*. He was not anti-Semitic, but he did not take pains to free himself from the anti-Semitism of his age. (Frighteningly, a particularly insensitive line in Chesterton's otherwise hilarious drinking song "The Logical Vegetarian" shows just how anti-Semitic a non-anti-Semite could be in his day.) He was no misogynist, but he did not go out of his way to advance the rights of women during this important period of women's suffrage. And some of his polemical writings are uncharitable. He converted from Anglicanism to Roman Catholicism in 1922 and, like some converts (for example, Thomas Merton, in his otherwise splendid *The Seven Storey Mountain*), his enthusiasm for his new faith went hand in glove with a failure to appreciate the merits of the communion he left.

Even so, his strengths were (like his size) huge. I highlight just three aspects of his writing: joy, the blending of imagination and ordinary, life-affirming values, and his sense of eternity. These were not simply topics he addressed; these were elements that shaped his style and composition of writing. The way he wrote, and what he wrote, are inextricably linked.

First off, it must be said that Chesterton wrote with joy, even when his topic was grievous. You can almost feel his pleasure in constructing his thoughts. As an example, consider the ending to the book *Orthodoxy:*

> Joy, which was the small publicity of the pagan, is the gigantic secret of the Christian. And as I close this chaotic volume I open again the strange small book from which all Christianity came; and I am again haunted by a kind of confirmation. The tremendous figure which fills the Gospels towers in this respect, as in every other, above all the thinkers who ever thought themselves tall. His pathos was natural, almost casual. The Stoics, ancient and modern, were proud of concealing their tears. He never concealed His tears; He showed them plainly on His open face at any daily sight, such as the far sight of His native city. Yet He concealed something. Solemn supermen and imperial diplomatists are proud of restraining their anger. He never restrained His anger. He flung furniture down the front steps of the Temple, and asked men how they expected to escape the damnation of hell. Yet He restrained something. I say it with reverence; there was in that shattering personality a thread that must be called shyness. There was something that He hid from all men when He went up a mountain to pray. There was something that He covered constantly by abrupt silence or impetuous isolation. There was some one thing that was too great for God to show us when He walked upon our earth; and I have sometimes fancied that it was His mirth.

That had to be written with a passionate joy. And I think it also testifies to Chesterton's overall approach to religion: "Let your religion be less of a theory and more of a love affair."

Second, Chesterton's imagination often wove together fantastic (in the sense of *grand* and, literally, *incredible*) imagery with an affirmation of domestic life and common sense. Here is a passage in which he asserts that, in the end, comradeship and friendship should be our chief goal rather than adventures abroad. But instead of stating this in explicit terms, he conjures up an extraordinary portrait taken from Dickens.

> But we have a long way to travel before we get back to what Dickens meant: and the passage is a long and rambling English road, a twisting road such as Mr. Pickwick traveled. But this at least is part of what he meant; that comradeship and serious joy are not interludes in our travel; but that our travels are interludes in comradeship and joy, which through God shall endure forever. The inn does not point to the road; the road points to the inn. And all roads point at last to an ultimate inn, where we shall meet Dickens and all his characters: and when we drink again it shall be from the great flagons in the tavern at the end of the world.

To take another example to fill out my suggestion, Chesterton wrote the delightful essay "Omar and the Sacred Vine" which is, essentially, a critique of both the temperance movement as well as a critique of drinking alcohol as a way to escape from the world. Rather than write something banal like "Be moderate in consuming alcohol," Chesterton pictures two great figures who offer you a drink: Omar Khayyam and Jesus Christ. This is the end of the essay:

Omar makes [wine], not a sacrament, but a medicine.
He feasts because life is not joyful; he revels because he
is not glad. "Drink," he says, "for you know not when
you go nor where. Drink, because the stars are cruel
and the world as idle as a humming top. Drink, because
there is nothing worth trusting, nothing worth fighting for. Drink, because all things are lapsed in a base
equality and an evil peace." So he stands offering us the
cup in his hand. And at the high altar of Christianity
stands another figure, in whose hand also is the cup of
the vine. "Drink" he says, "for the whole world is as red
as this wine, with the crimson of the love and wrath
of God. Drink, for the trumpets are blowing for battle
and this is the stirrup-cup. Drink, for this is my blood
of the new testament that is shed for you. Drink, for I
know of whence you come and why. Drink, for I know
of when you go and where."

As for the third and final virtue of his work to highlight
here, I believe you can find Chesterton's sense of the eternal
throughout much of his writing—poetry, detective fiction, novels, literary criticism, and so on. But it is often most poignant
in the essays in which he takes on some theme or incident and
then builds on it in order to gesture to that which goes well
beyond the moment. Consider "A Defence of Rash Vows."
Chesterton begins by listing a host of what we would consider
nonsense—chaining two mountains together in the Alps, for
example. When you conclude the essay you might be (or at least
I am) convinced that such an act would be one of the most sane
acts to undertake despite the fact (as Chesterton notes at the
outset) that "a mountain is commonly a stationary and reliable
object which it is not necessary to chain up at night like a dog."
His thesis is that his age was slipping into a time of malleability

and cowardice, where someone might offer a dramatic vow of love, for example, and seek to gain the luster from such a proclamation yet completely lack the character or energy to fulfill the vow.

> The man who makes a vow makes an appointment with himself at some distant time or place. The danger of it is that he himself should not keep the appointment. And in modern times this terror of one's self, of the weakness and mutability of one's self, has perilously increased. . . . And the end of all this is that maddening horror of unreality which descends upon the decadents, and compared with which physical pain itself would have the freshness of a youthful thing.

I will give Chesterton the last word in sketching his "argument" or case for vows over against what he sees as a tired and decadent approach to promises and our sense of our own identity. I use quotation marks around the word argument because I believe Chesterton is weaving a spell, or breaking one spell and introducing another, rather than developing something purely logical or rationally compelling on formal grounds. One word of explanation in order to set up the context for the passage that follows: there is an old saying in military strategy to the effect that you should not corner a desperate army. There is also the reverse wisdom: if you are a commander and you require for your army to fight with desperation, you might allow the army to be cornered or, perhaps more dramatically, you might cut off all escape for the troops by, say, destroying your ships.

> There are thrilling moments, doubtless, for the spectator, the amateur, and the ascetic; but there is one thrill that is known only to the soldier who fights for his own

flag, to the ascetic who starves himself for his own
illumination, to the lover who makes finally his own
choice. And it is this transfiguring self-discipline that
makes the vow a truly sane thing. It must have satisfied
even the giant hunger of the soul of a lover or a poet
to know that in consequence of some instant of decision that strange chain would hang for centuries in the
Alps among the silences of stars and snows. All around
us is the city of small sins, abounding in backways and
retreats, but surely, sooner or later, the towering flame
will rise from the harbour announcing that the reign of
the cowards is over and a man is burning his ships.

The Virtues of the Cloister

THE VICTORIAN ERA (1837–1901) IN GREAT BRITAIN, AND the fact that Britain was the largest European imperial power throughout much of the world, resulted in periods of dramatic conflict: the inclusion of India into the British Empire, war in Afghanistan, the Crimean War between Russia and Britain, the Boer War, the Opium Wars, the tragic famine and the battle for home rule in Ireland, and so on. There were also immense social hardships as Great Britain entered the industrial age. In the midst of all this, a priest in the Church of England, Richard Meux Benson, founded a monastic order, first called the Cowley Brotherhood (Cowley is a city near Oxford) and then the Society of St. John the Evangelist (SSJE).

Two hundred years earlier the poet John Milton famously condemned virtues that are untested. He employed a monastic image to make his point, likening the cloister to a place of retreat and passivity.

> I cannot praise a fugitive and cloistered virtue, unexercised and unbreathed, that never sallies out and sees her adversary, but slinks out of the race, where that immortal garland is to be run for, not without dust and heat . . . that which purifies us is trial, and trial is by what is contrary.

I believe there is much to Milton's main thesis about untested "virtues" (it would be hard to call someone courageous if he or she were never faced with danger) but his assumption about the cloister seems open to question.

When Father Benson established the community based on the testimony of Saint John ("the beloved disciple"), he did an extraordinary act: he dug deeply into the Christian tradition and laid claim to the abundant life Jesus promised, life that comes from abiding in him so that we may know of the overwhelming love from the Father through the work of the Holy Spirit. "The world's madness will hurry on its own ruin," wrote Father Benson, "but the seed of God shall abide safely." Benson understood the monastic life as one that is not merely natural or congenial:

> No outward troubles can master us if we are but true
> to the Life of God in our own selves. That life will
> assert itself in all our ministry. No circumstances can
> be unfavourable to that which is supernatural.

Benson and the community he founded were a vital, stable reference point during the religious upheaval of the time: the challenges to the Church of England from the re-emergence of Roman Catholicism, the growing protestant nonconformists, and the increased secularity of culture, politics, and education. And as the order grew with a religious community in Boston and then Cambridge, there was a pronounced movement to minister to the poor and marginalized. There was a great link between the cloister and the street, between meditation in solitude and making arrangements to lodge the homeless. My own first encounter with this monastic order was in precisely such terms.

In the late 1970s in Boston, the Episcopal Church of St. John the Evangelist was served by the SSJE. The church had a reputation for high liturgy and social outreach. We had a regular soup kitchen service every Thursday. This sometimes hosted as few as sixty people, and sometimes well over a hundred. One of the priests from the order who was often there was Father David Clayton. Father Clayton was superb in the cloister as well as on the street. In the cloister, he was especially good in encouraging an inner integrity and centering. During one retreat at the monastery, I found a passage from the work of Gustave Thibon very useful; it captured much of Father Clayton's spirit.

> You feel you are hedged in; you dream of escape; but beware of mirages. Do not run or fly away in order to get free; rather dig in the narrow place which has been given you; you will find God there and everything. God does not float on our horizon, he sleeps in your substance. Vanity runs, love digs. If you fly away from yourself, your prison will run with you and will close in because of the wind of your flight; if you go deep down into yourself it will disappear in paradise.

This interior digging was not something narrowly introspective, however. Father Clayton's theology linked an inner wholeness with external action. This came home to me during a vexing evening when our church was serving around a hundred people (mostly indigents) dinner.

That Thursday, I was cleaning dishes. Father Clayton came up to me. "Look what I have!" Father Clayton looked excited— in a good, not panic-stricken matter. He opened his coat to reveal a large knife.

"Father Clayton! Where did you get this?" I exclaimed.

"I got it from a young man," he replied. "I told him I would return it to him after the meal." And Father Clayton walked off (though it would be more accurate to say that he skipped off) to look after some of our other guests.

I did not see Father Clayton get or give back the knife, though as I left the church I saw him talking with a young man in a little side chapel. I don't know what was said, so I cannot bring this brief account to a close.

Except to say what I suspect: Getting that knife from the young man probably was made easier after years of prayer and self-examination in the cloister.

PART THREE

Divine Love

It's Waterloo, Baby!

"I CAN'T LIVE AND I CAN'T DIE." MY FATHER, 94 YEARS old and recovering from a stroke, told me this twice over the Thanksgiving Holiday. I tried to cheer him up by reading him eyewitness accounts of great battles. The Battle of Agincourt in 1415 was alright, but he was more impressed by the Napoleonic wars, especially the Battle of Trafalgar and Waterloo. "Poor Lord Nelson," my father sighed, as I read about his death on October 21, 1805, at the end of the decisive British naval victory over the French. In his final hours, Lord Nelson asked Captain Hardy to look after Lady Hamilton (his mistress), saying, "Hardy: take care of poor Lady Hamilton. Kiss me, Hardy." According to Dr. William Beatty, "The Captain now knelt down, and kissed his cheek; when his Lordship said, 'Now I am satisfied. Thank God, I have done my duty.'"

At this point at my parents' home, there is a strange blend of distress, resignation, and family love. However, on that day, just to make sure things are as they seemed I had to ask, "Dad, is there a Lady Hamilton you would like to tell me about?" I wanted a heads up if some day DNA testing would reveal that I have a second family or if, at the funeral, my mother might have to confront a mysterious "companion." Dad assured me that he was not in Nelson's league, and we then went on reading about the extraordinary charge of the Scots Greys and 92nd

Highlanders at Waterloo, on June 18, 1815. Dad said something about how he was facing his own Waterloo.

"England expects that every man this day will do his duty." These were the famous words that Lord Nelson sent out to his fleet just before the sea battle at Trafalgar. I often think, "St. Olaf College expects everyone to do his or her duty," when I am in great distress in class, such as when students presented me with a video in which a photograph of me is stapled to a banana and there is a subsequent narrative where I "rescue" an action elf (Legolas from the movie sequence *The Lord of the Rings*). This happened at the end of a course in Aesthetics, and the film, in keeping with course themes, was "creative," but unsettling. Wandering a cold corridor back to my office, I wondered whether the semester had utterly collapsed into a theatre of absurdity.

Another incriminating event: just after Halloween a student appeared dressed as me (gray hair, loose tie, etc.) mimicking all my ridiculous mannerisms. The event was funny and not the fruit of contempt and loathing, but it also drove home (with conviction and clarity) a very simple, easily stated self-awareness: I am absurd. For some reason, there have been a score of similar "difficult moments" this fall. Somehow, thinking of Nelson and duty helps in these situations. I recommend it.

But, fortunately, saying goodbye to my parents this Thanksgiving did not feel like a duty—though near the end I did think of Nelson. There was even a bit of humor on Dad's part.

"I'm not dead yet. Sorry to disappoint you," Dad said, and then he kissed me and Jil on the cheek so very, very tenderly. As I drove to the airport, I wasn't thinking of battles. My mind went back to a Patristic meditation on "the kiss of peace" and the sacraments. As I recall, the conclusion of this meditation is that whether in the midst of earthly victory or defeat, the kiss of peace and the sacraments are a sign of something transcendent, something immortal or eternal. I believe the exact words are: "Such a loving kiss is the medicine of immortality." As we were heading out the driveway I shouted out to my father, "Lord Nelson has nothing on you."

It's the Siege of Stalingrad, Darling!

———•———

AT FIRST I THOUGHT MY FATHER SAID SOMETHING ABOUT the scourge of Satan or the search for graduates. While either might make a little sense (earlier I had been reading to him Milton's *Paradise Lost,* and we talked recently about how I will miss students when they graduate in May), I was at a loss for how to respond. A hospice nurse clued me in: "Darling. Your father is trying to tell you that he wants you to read to him about the siege of Stalingrad."

It was not immediately obvious to me why someone who would turn 95 next Thursday, and who had been told by our family doctor that he has less than six months to live, wanted to be read historical accounts of eighteen months of urban warfare in Russia. Dad was active as a pilot in World War II, flying between the U.S. and the U.K., and he got further east in 1948–49 when he participated in the Berlin Airlift, a successful campaign by Western Allies to thwart the Soviet Union's ambition to achieve total domination over West Berlin. But as far as I can tell, Dad has no direct experience of Stalingrad, that Soviet industrial center on the Volga River that the German army unsuccessfully assaulted, beginning in the summer of 1942.

Up until now, Dad has enjoyed thinking about history and current foreign affairs. In light of our most recent conversations, I suggested that Justinian (527–565), the last of the great Roman Emperors, was more on topic under present circumstances than the Red Army and some panzer divisions. There are some interesting parallels between Justinian and our current state of affairs, internationally and nationally. Justinian launched an expensive military campaign based on faulty intelligence. A study of Justinian by the Bush administration would have drawn attention to the danger of relying too heavily on the testimony of exiles; they sometimes give you an exaggerated portrait of their own importance and a diminished view of the obstacles standing in the way of returning them to their homeland and putting them back in power. Justinian also had problems with Persia, though this involved buying a negotiated peace from Shah Chosroes I of Persia (531–579) rather than military occupation. Like Bush, Justinian was loved and hated, and he also sought to bring together (in today's terminology) "communities of faith" to bolster cultural harmony.

But quite apart from any religious, military, or political links to our present times, I thought Dad would relish Justinian's architectural and artistic achievements. The Christianity of his day was a religion of interiors, both spiritual and architectural. Spiritually, there was an emphasis on the relation of the soul and God, and, in terms of physical space, believers often met in private houses rather than in magnificent temples or in public procession. It was in Justinian's reign that a dramatic shift was made to stunning, expansive interiors like the great church Hagia Sophia (Holy Wisdom)—which is still standing as the largest dome in Istanbul.

But for Dad, now, such big spaces with their frescoes and mosaics are not interesting or of central interest. Even finding historical analogies between Ancient or Medieval history and current politics seems tedious. Dad can barely get out of a chair without aid. His "world," physically, has shrunk to a few rooms. Dad's mind seems more interior, more intent than ever on finding some kind of spiritual footing amid the kind of confusion, noise, and struggle that you would find in a narrow street fight.

One of my friends cajoles me, "Did someone tell you the end was going to be nice?" The friend observes that if I thought my dad would end his days with mirth and laughter, I was wrong, wrong, wrong. He cites the seventeenth-century French philosopher Pascal: "The last act is bloody, however fine the rest of the play. They throw earth over your head and it is finished." But Pascal did not think the end of one's earthly life was the absolute end of the soul; he had an ecstatic vision of God which he recorded in three words. These were found after his death stitched into the lining of his coat: Feeling. Joy. Peace. *(Sentiment. Joie. Paix).* By Pascal's lights, the feelings of vibrancy, joy, and peace we have in this world may be signs of a greater arena in which the soul finds its home in God. Evelyn Underhill comments on the experience of Pascal and others, "Consciousness has suddenly changed its rhythm and a new aspect of the universe rushes in. The teasing mists are swept away, and reveal, if only for an instant, the Everlasting Hills."

At present, feelings of vibrancy, joy, and peace are difficult for my family. We pray for my father to have as much joy and serenity as possible under the circumstances, and as much faith as possible in a joy that is, in Dorothy Sayers' words, deeper and more powerful than the grave. Yes, I would prefer that Dad and I were strolling around a grand, serene basilica with life-affirming mosaics. Regrettably, life right now is just too boxed in for any of that, and comfort must instead be found in stories of the costly virtues that are won when things look desperate and not at all serene or life-affirming. Did the hospice nurse somehow know beforehand that dying patients routinely ask for histories of World War II battles? After all, despite the wickedness of Stalin (who was as wicked as Milton's Satan in *Paradise Lost*), the Battle of Stalingrad was an Allied victory; it prevented the German Army from getting the oil supply from the Caucasus and, ultimately, it turned the tide against Hitler in the East. Agreed, now is not the time to read to Dad stories of Justinian, not even stories of his enormously interesting relationship with his wife, the mysterious empress Theodora. It's the siege of Stalingrad, darling. But if Pascal is right, by the grace of God, the soul's final destiny is joy, not siege warfare and the silence of the grave.

Love. Love. Love.

———•———

FOR A LONG TIME, I DID NOT THINK MY PARENTS WERE mortal. Once, in a conversation with a friend, I said, "If my parents die. . . ." My friend interrupted: "'If'? You must have very strong parents!"

Near the end, the books my dad requested that we read together left little doubt about the facts of mortality. Last fall we read eyewitness accounts of the Napoleonic wars. In the winter Dad wanted to take on histories of the successful defense of the city of Stalingrad against the German assault that ended in February 1943. Our last excursion involved submarine warfare in the Pacific during the same war.

There is an enormous literature on dying, death, and grieving. There is probably even a handbook: *The Idiot's Guide to Death*. But none that I have read so far highlight the importance of reading about battles or, more specifically, submarine crews. I suspect, however, that in my dad's final year, at 95, after a stroke and confined to a bed, he had great empathy with those who lived in cramped conditions and tried to dodge torpedoes and depth charges. He seemed equally interested in the lives of the hunted and the hunters, of submarines on the attack and in defense, as well as the anti-submarine tactics involving radar and noisemakers (a tactical diversion noisemaker is attached to the rear of a ship designed to guide torpedoes away from the ship's hull.) Three weeks ago, he requested that the reading stop, and conversation became difficult.

There are wonderful poems and images of entering the next life by ship. When St. Paul writes of his longing to leave this life for the hereafter with Christ, the Greek term for "leaving" is the same for "lifting anchor." I am not acquainted with any works that describe entering the next life in a submarine, but in *The Divine Comedy* there is a passage in which Dante travels toward paradise through purgatory almost completely submerged in water.

Whatever your favorite poetic vehicle (I am fond of Elijah going to heaven in a chariot with horses of fire), there is a resilient Christian tradition that the way to heaven must be through love. In the English spiritual manual *The Cloud of Unknowing* there is some simple, interesting advice on approaching God through periods of trial, which the author pictures as a great cloud. The writer (anonymous) recommends that whenever you feel lost in the search for God, you should repeat the words "love" or "God" a lot; both words amount to the same thing, for "God is love" (1 John 4:8). "This word [love] shall be your shield and your spear whether you ride in peace or in war. With the word 'love' you shall beat upon the cloud and the darkness, which are above you. With this word you shall strike down thoughts of every kind and drive them beneath the cloud of forgetting." In the end, love must take precedence over all other thoughts and emotions: "God may be reached and held close by means of love, but by means of thought never."

Two weeks before he died, Dad and I had the following exchange. I said: "I really love you, Daddy." He said: "Don't make me cry." Neither of us cried. We held hands. "You know, Dad, when you get to the other side, there might be lots of questions. I hear that it's a good idea to say the word 'love' a lot." He squeezed my hand three times and said:

"Love. Love. Love."

Notes

I articulate and defend some of the philosophy that is in play throughout this book in *Consciousness and the Mind of God* (Cambridge: Cambridge University Press, 1994). You may also find it in my *Evidence and Faith: Philosophy and Religion Since the Seventeenth Century* (Cambridge: Cambridge University Press, 2005); *Contemporary Philosophy of Religion* (Oxford: Blackwell, 1998); *Praying with C. S. Lewis* (Winona, Minn.: St. Mary's Press, 1998); and the collection *Cambridge Platonist Spirituality*, co-edited by C. Taliaferro and Alison Tepley (New York: Paulist Press, 2004).

Citations from the Bible, Shakespeare, Milton, and some poetry are given in the text, and not repeated here.

An Introduction
The passage from the work of Hugh of St. Victor is taken from the magnificent study *Love in Twelfth Century France* by J. C. Moore (Philadelphia: University of Pennsylvania Press, 1972), 154–156.

G. K. Chesterton, "Wings of Stone," in *Alarms and Discursions* (New York: Mead & Company, 1911).

Do Not Hug a Tree on a Job Interview
Unless There Is a Very Good Reason for Doing So
C. S. Lewis, *The Allegory of Love* (Oxford: Oxford University Press, 1938), 196.

Drugs, a Bear, and an Owl: A Testimony

Aldous Huxley, *The Doors of Perception* (London: Chatto & Windus, 1954).

I Want to Hold Your Hand!

William McNeill, *Plagues and People* (New York: Doubleday, 1972).

I Am So Sorry!

Richard Swinburne, *Responsibility and Atonement* (Oxford: Clarendon Press, 1998).

Gabrielle Taylor, *Pride, Shame, and Guilt* (Oxford: Oxford University Press, 1985).

Hilary Mantel, *A Change of Climate* (New York: Henry Holt & Co., 1997).

The Knights of the Round Table in the American Colonies

Sir Gawain and the Green Knight, trans. Brian Stone (Harmondsworth: Penguin Books, 1974).

A Student's Tale

Charles Williams, "Taliessin on the Death of Virgil," in *Taliessin through Logres* (Oxford: Oxford University Press, 1969), 31–32.

Confessions of a Sleep Walker

G. K. Chesterton, *Charles Dickens: A Critical Study* (New York: Mead & Company, 1926) chapter 2.

The Goblins and My Parents

Nathaniel Hawthorne, "A Bundle of Letters," *The Portable Hawthorne* (New York: The Viking Press, Inc., 1969), 672.

John Bunyan, *The Pilgrim's Progress* (New York: New American Library, 1964), 106–109.

Are We in a Crisis Yet?

Gustave Flaubert, *Sentimental Education*, Robert Baldrich trans. (Harmondsworth: Penguin Classics, 1964), 286.

Love from Afar

My presentation to the NSF conference was revised (radically) and later published in *Life Science Ethics*, ed. G. Comstock (Ames: Iowa State University, 2002).

Lady Wisdom

William Langland, *Piers the Ploughman*, trans. J. F. Goodride (Harmondsworth: Penguin, 1966) 36–37.

Cloud of Unknowing, trans. Ira Progoff (New York: Delta Books, 1957), 66.

Denis de Rougemont, *Love in the Western World* (New York: Harper Colophon, 1956), 15.

The Consolations of Philosophy, ed. I. Edman (New York: Modern Library, 1943), 115–116.

Still Standing?

My presentation was later written up and is published with co-author Anders Hendrickson as "Hume's Racism and the Case against Miracles," *Philosophia Christi* 4, no. 2 (2003): 427–441.

Moving Images

G. K. Chesterton, *G. F. Watts* (London: Duckworth, 1904), 88.

The view of imagination I resist is set forth in the early sections of Colin McGinn's *Mindsight* (Cambridge, Mass.: Harvard University Press, 2004).

M. K. Gandhi, *An Autobiography or The Story of My Experiments with Truth*, trans. M. Desai (Ahmedabad: Navajiran Publishing House, 1972), xi.

Denis de Rougemont, *Love in the Western World*, 145.

Be Nice!

Thucydides, *History of the Peloponnesian War*, trans. R. Warner (London: Penguin, 1972), 220, 221, 229, 401–408.

Prayer and Foreign Policy

James Rusling, "Interview with President William McKinley," *The Christian Advocate* (22 January 1903), 17.

Dying on Campaign

Herodotus, *Histories,* trans. Robin Waterfield (Oxford: Oxford University Press, 1998).

From Russia with Faith, Hope, and Love

The proceedings of the conference on the Trinity are published under the title *The Trinity: East-West Dialogue,* ed. Melville Stewart (Dordrecht: Kluwer, 2003).

Leo Tolstoy, *The Cossacks and Other Stories,* "The Death of Ivan Ilyich" (New York: Penguin Books Ltd., 1960), 159–161.

Racism and the Woods

Evelyn Waugh, *Brideshead Revisited* (Boston: Little, Brown & Co., 1945), 288.

Now *That* Is an Interesting Machine Gun

Augustine of Hippo, *The City of God.* trans. G. W. Walsh (Garden City: Image Books, 1953), Book xix, chapter xii.

A Modest Defense of Magic

T. H. White, *The Book of Merlyn* (Austin: University of Texas Press, 1977), xv.

Enemies Are at the Gate, but Friends Are at the Door!

J. R. R. Tolkien, *The Two Towers* (New York: Ballantine Books, 1965), chapters 6–7.

The Passion and the Happiness of the Christ

J. R. R. Tolkien, *The Return of the King* (New York: Ballantine Books, 1965), 283.

J. R. R. Tolkien, "On Fairy Stories" in *The Tolkien Reader* by J. R. R. Tolkien (New York: Ballantine Books, 1966), 68.

Is the Detective Chief Inspector in Love Today?

W. H. Auden, "The Guilty Vicarage," in *The Dryer's Hand and Other Essays* (London: Faber, 1963), 146–158.

Going Up? The Lighter Side of Christian Mysticism

This story of St. Teresa is taken from *The Way of the Mystics,* J. M. Talbot and S. Rabey (San Francisco: Jossey-Bass, 2005), 128.

St. Teresa of Avila, *The Way of Perfection,* trans. and ed. E. A. Peers (New York: Image Books, 1964), 75–76.

A Very Large, Magical Victorian

G. K. Chesterton, "Joy," in *Orthodoxy* (London: John Lane, 1919), chapter IX.

G. K. Chesterton, *Charles Dickens,* Part II (London: Methuen, 1906), chapter XII.

G. K. Chesterton, "Omar and the Sacred Vine," in *Heretics* (New York: John Lane Co., 1905)

G. K. Chesterton, "A Defence of Rash Vows," in *The Defendant* (London: J.M. Dent & Sons, Ltd., 1902).

The Virtues of the Cloister

See *Letters of Richard Meux Benson, SSJE* (London: A.F. Mowbray, 1916).

Gustave Thibon, cited by Gabriel Marcel in *Homo Viator,* ed. E. Craufurd (London: Victor Gollancz, 1951), 28.

John Milton, *Areopagitica and Of Education* (Arlington Heights, Ill.: Harlan Davidson, Inc. 1951).

Love. Love. Love.

The Cloud of Unknowing, 72–73, 77.